21
MYTHS
THAT CAN
WRECK
YOUR
MARRIAGE

Other Books by Barbara Russell Chesser

Because You Care: Practical Ideas for Helping Those Who Grieve

Building Family Strengths: Blueprints for Action, Volume I (co-editor)

Building Family Strengths: Blueprints for Action, Volume II (co-editor)

Child Guidance

Marriage—Creating a Partnership (co-author)

Improving Graduate Programs for Developing Countries

The Role of Women in International Development

21 MYTHS THAT CAN WRECK YOUR MARRIAGE

BARBARA RUSSELL CHESSER

WORD PUBLISHING

Dallas · London · Vancouver · Melbourne

21 MYTHS THAT CAN WRECK YOUR MARRIAGE: HOW A COUPLE CAN AVOID HEAD-ON COLLISIONS

Scripture quotations used in this book are from the following sources:

The King James Version of the Bible (KJV).

The Modern Language Bible (MLB), The Berkeley Version in Modern English. Copyright © 1945, 1959, 1969 by Zondervan Publishing House. Used by permission.

The New American Standard Bible (NASB), © 1960, 1962, 1963, 1968, 1971, 1972, 1973, 1975, 1977 by The Lockman Foundation. Used by permission.

The Revised Standard Version of the Bible (RSV), copyrighted 1946, 1952, © 1971, 1973 by the Division of Christian Education of the National Council of the Churches of Christ in the U.S.A. Used by permission.

The Living Bible (TLB), copyright © 1971 by Tyndale House Publishers, Wheaton, IL. Used by permission.

This book is about real people; names and identifying information in some cases have been changed to protect confidentiality. All people have granted permission for their stories to be told; any resemblance to any other individual is purely coincidental.

Library of Congress Cataloging-in-Publication Data

Chesser, Barbara.
    21 myths that can wreck your marriage : how a couple can avoid head-on collisions / Barbara Russell Chesser.
        p.   cm.
    ISBN 0-8499-0820-5—ISBN 0-8499-3161-4 (pbk.)
    1. Marriage—United States. 2. Marriage—Religious aspects—Christianity.   I. Title.   II. Title: Twenty-one myths that can wreck your marriage.
HQ734.C545   1990
306.85—dc20   90-31418
                                                     CIP

Printed in the United States of America

0 1 2 3 4 9 AGF 9 8 7 6 5 4 3 2

To Del and Christi
and
the larger circle of
family and friends
who have provided me with
a gratifying life
filled with lots of love
and laughter

CONTENTS

FOREWORD

"Things are not what they seem" is a line poets, playwrights, and humorists apply to a wide variety of people and predicaments. Nowhere are these words more fitting than with marriage. Baffling myths, illusions, misconceptions, false assumptions, and other shaky notions about marriage leave countless husbands and wives in a chronic state of confusion, disappointment, and disillusionment. Many of these fallacies are so deeply entrenched in our thinking that they enjoy the status of Holy Writ.

Although marriage is considered to be one of society's most potentially rewarding and satisfying relationships, it proves also to be one of the most complex and perplexing. Few universal, never-fail rules exist for "living happily ever after." What makes for a convivial relationship for one couple may destroy the intimacy for another. What works once for a particular couple fails them at another time or in a different situation. What to one marriage partner is certain to guarantee holy wedlock to the other spells holy deadlock. Even the experts do not agree. What one advocates for marital bliss another says causes marital blahs.

"You shall know the truth and the truth shall set you free." Not limited to our spiritual life, these timeless words strike a chord when referring to marriage today. More than ever, marriage cries out for sincerity, genuineness, honesty, integrity, trust, and other vital elements of truth. *21 Myths That Can Wreck Your Marriage* sheds light and levity—and truth—on some of the damaging myths and paradoxes plaguing the hallowed institution of marriage today. This book's warmth and wisdom-packed pages will give those preparing for marriage some forewarning, the confused some clarity, the uptight some relaxation, the discouraged some encouragement, the miserable some relief, and the complacent something to think about.

Barbara Russell Chesser is uniquely qualified to write this book that shatters some of our most cherished beliefs about marriage. She possesses real-life qualities searched for by the make-believe *Wizard of Oz* characters Dorothy met in her sojourn to the City of Oz—a brain, heart, and courage. With her brains, Barbara has always been able to go right to the core of a matter, whether in research, teaching, or counseling situations. And that quality shines unmistakably in *21 Myths That Can Wreck Your Marriage.* Instead of the arcane psychobabble and verbose treatises on theories that bore us all, the words Barbara uses in this book make for interesting, thought-provoking, curl-up-on-the-couch reading.

Barbara also has a heart for people and an engaging transparency. The pulse of Barbara's heart for people and her authenticity are felt throughout the pages of this book as she shares stories of people and their struggles to go beyond false-face smiles, to shed facades, and to free themselves from fallacies that rob marriage of its richness.

Barbara's courage is evidenced by her commitment to write this book. The enormity of the task is incomprehensible—the poring over voluminous notes and case studies, the agonizing decisions about what to share out of one's own experience and innermost reflections, and then the sheer mental torture of making sense out of the madness and getting the words right to add meaning to marriage.

Not only blessed with brains, heart, and courage, Barbara also possesses the rare quality of demonstrating in her own life and marriage the truths about which she writes.

An ancient proverb says, "You must study the map, but you won't get any closer to the city until you start moving." I invite you—urge you—to read Barbara Russell Chesser's book. Start moving today toward a more rewarding relationship by applying some of this book's insights to your

marriage. Put into practice this seed of truth brought to
life in *21 Myths That Can Wreck Your Marriage:*

> Those who love the truth
> Must seek love in marriage,
> Love without illusions.

John DeFrain, Ph.D.
Department of Human Development
and the Family
University of Nebraska-Lincoln

MYTH 1:

All You Need Is Love

A CYNIC ONCE SAID, "Marriage is like a hot bath. Once you get used to it, it ain't so hot." I take exception to part of this dour skeptic's point of view. Anyone knows if the bath water gets too cold, you merely add more hot water. Yet we often fail to use this same common sense in marriage. We think, perhaps subconsciously, that on our wedding day all we need is enough love for each other, and our marriage will last a lifetime, propelling us through all the marital storms that life might blow our way. Erroneously, we believe that after we "tie the knot," we will automatically, effortlessly live in marital bliss "till death do us part." This is a dangerous myth, and anyone who lives by this fanciful notion is likely to live instead in marital blahs.

The time-tested saying, "An ounce of prevention is worth a pound of cure," applies to keeping the fire aflame in marriage just as it applies to taking a good, long, hot soaking bath. Just sitting there listlessly hoping things will improve does not get the job done. You need to add more hot water *before* the entire tub cools off. One essential step in preventing marriage from cooling off is getting rid of unrealistic expectations for marriage, or what I call the "cure-all fantasy."

The Cure-All Fantasy

Growing up in New Mexico, I enjoyed accompanying relatives to a resort town nestled in scenic mountains near a crystal clear lake. My relatives from the high, dry, hot plains of eastern New Mexico were drawn there by the cool air, the refreshing smell of pine trees, and the good fishing. But what captured my fascination were the crowds of people trekking there because of the allure of the hot springs touted to cure virtually any malady that ailed you. Individuals with every affliction imaginable besieged the "bath houses" in desperate search of a miraculous cure-all.

A drive through that little town last year stirred up childhood memories—the cool air, the smell of pine trees, and the good fishing were all still there. As for the throngs of hopeful people, they had dwindled years ago, according to an oldtimer. Their hopes for a cure-all were dashed against the unyielding wall of reality; they had expected more than the springs could deliver. A lot of people hold similar unrealistic expectations of marriage. They believe if they just have enough love at the beginning of their marriage, that their mate and the marriage itself will meet every need, assuage every disappointment, soothe every frustration, and heal every hurt. Like the people soaking in the hot springs, they simply expect too much.

In his book *How to Keep a Good Thing Going*, John W. Drakeford says the characteristics of romantic love are based mostly on emotions that often cause irrational and irresponsible behavior. The very language of romantic love reflects its psychotic nature, which tends to immobilize people. For example, he is "crazy" about her; she is "mad" about him.

In contrast, mature love, the kind that provides a foundation on which a strong marriage can be built and which energizes the partners, is not based solely on emotions but on a way of *acting*, a method and manner of treating our loved objects. Stripped of the cure-all fantasy of romantic love, rational individuals do not depend on the ephemeral emotions of love to sustain their marriage. Instead, they know they must *learn* to love and to carry out the actions of love as spelled out in this time-proven passage:

> Love is very patient and kind, never jealous or envious, never boastful or proud, never haughty or selfish or rude. Love does not demand its own way. It is not irritable or touchy. It does not hold grudges and will hardly even notice when others do it wrong. It is never glad about injustice, but rejoices whenever truth wins out. If you love someone you will be loyal to him no matter what the cost. You will always believe in him, always expect the best of him, and always stand your ground in defending him. (1 Cor. 13:4–7, TLB)

Keeping the Temperature Right

The coming together in marriage of two people with distinct personalities is like the meeting of two mountain streams. The two lives rush against each other. Personalities and preferences clash. Habits vie for position. Ideas contend for power. Sometimes, like two roaring streams after a spring cloud burst, confrontations overwhelm everything in their path, leaving the feuding partners wondering where the romance has gone. Or, as Sylvia Harney put it in *Married Beyond Recognition:* "Romance is like a paper lantern left standing out in the rain. After awhile the light goes out and you're left with a soggy, plain brown bag."

The authors of *A New Look at Love* describe the pattern this way:

> All newlyweds are romantic. The man is fiery, impetuous, and tender. The woman is soft, shy, and blooming. Somehow, in just a very few years, all that changes. The impetuous man turns into a dull, plodding businessman happier with his newspaper than with his wife. The blooming woman turns into a sharp-tongued shrew. We're all familiar with this dismal view of marriage and, to some degree, accept it as true.[1]

Wait a minute! This isn't the marriage you had in mind. But by now you may be getting the picture that a good marriage needs more than a big rush of romantic love at its inception. It may sound contradictory, but actually the more realistic you are, the more romance you can enjoy throughout your marriage. Just recognize that a marriage soon gets stagnant if neglected, that warm feelings for each other cool off if ignored, and relationships are wrecked not by a blowout but rather by a slow leak. So, to keep your marriage from cooling off, try the following suggestions:

1. *Make a commitment to each other to rekindle the flame.* Don't just try to avoid the quicksand of divorce, but strive to have an *enjoyable* relationship. Make your commitment to the relationship not just to the marriage. To keep warm feelings for each other, use the same courtesy and kindness you usually extend to complete strangers. Daily practice in the following short course in human relations will help:

> The six most important words:
> *I admit I made a mistake.*
> The five most important words:
> *You did a good job.*
> The four most important words:
> *What is your opinion?*
> The three most important words:
> *I love you.*
> The two most important words:
> *Thank you.*
> The one most important word:
> *We.*

Commitment to each other and to your relationship may mean simply keeping yourselves attractive to each other. Beauty may be only skin deep, but good grooming and making the most of your looks never cooled off a marriage. As a wise old farmer once observed, "If the barn needs painting, paint it."

2. *Care enough to risk making positive changes in the marriage.* Sometimes couples spend years not rocking the marital boat. But some change is generally required if a

marriage is to survive. In *How Not to Ruin a Perfectly Good Marriage*, the authors point out:

> Change is the constant in any relationship. It is inevitable, necessary. And it *will* occur, for good or bad, no matter what you do. Resistance itself is action and will produce a response, a change, in the other person. You can't fight it. So the key is to recognize change, welcome it, and grow from it. As individuals grow and develop, they, of necessity, change.[2]

Change, to be sure, is frightening, especially when it involves two married individuals, because no guarantees are provided on the outcome. No assurances are given that both partners will change together or in the same direction. That is where commitment to each other and to the relationship comes in, and the myth that "all you need is love" goes out. To survive these inevitable changes spouses must be committed to encourage each other to grow, and committed to understand, to respect, to avoid feeling threatened, and to stand by each other. Changes may entail small, minor adjustments; or they may involve large significant ones, like changing jobs, moving to another city, or changing career directions.

"Change may be painful because it threatens our security, our predictable way of doing things," says one middle-aged wife who has admittedly struggled to see the positive aspects of moving numerous times to accommodate her husband's corporate career. "But all the give and take, and all the sharing, and all the willingness to support each other," she emphasizes, "is what makes a marriage dynamic, vital—and lasting!"

3. Build mutual understanding. Every time I unwrap a bar of Ivory soap, and see the words "It floats," I chuckle, remembering a lesson in communication. Several years ago, so a story goes, someone was asked to write advertising copy for a new product. This is what he wrote:

> The alkaline element and fats in this product are combined in such a manner so as to provide the highest quality of

suponification together with a specific gravity that keeps it
afloat on top of the water thereby relieving bathers the
trouble and annoyance of fishing around for it in the bottom of their bath water in their ablutions.

The bewildered boss read these words and asked, "What
does this mean?"

"It floats," was the reply.

The boss remarked in astonishment, "Why didn't you just
say that in the first place?"

To build mutual understanding in marriage, learn to say
what you mean. Beating around the bush, expecting your
mate to read your mind, or using unfair tactics like the
silent treatment all obstruct mutual understanding!

In the book *Marriage Personalities*, David Field gives a
good example of what I mean: A wife may say, "I would like
to go out to dinner with you, but I feel a little afraid and
embarrassed because I think it is improper to ask, since it's
my birthday." She could have said, "You forgot my birthday
again!" or "You never take me out to eat. You even expect
me to cook on my birthday!" But these statements put her
husband on the defensive. By using, "I" statements, she lets
him know what she wants, feels, and thinks, but allows her
husband to choose his response.[3]

4. *"Keep your eyes . . . half shut."* In marriage we are
much like a person stripped naked for a hot bath. We
are seen as we really are. We are no longer protected by the
masks we wear for the rest of the world—we see all
the faults and failings of each other. And when the marital
gears jam, we sometimes grow strangely sensitive to abra-
sive habits and idiosyncracies we hardly noticed before. To
keep the marriage from becoming as painful as a hot bath
on a new sunburn, we need to avoid pointing out each
other's every flaw and foible. Most of us are already
acutely aware of them!

In *Learning to Live with the People You Love*, James
Kennedy tells the story about a man who walked all the
way from New York to California. At the end of the journey,
he was asked if he ever thought he was not going to make it.

His answer: "Many times." When asked what had almost defeated him, he said that it wasn't the ice-tipped mountains of the Rockies or the blazing sun over the desert but rather over and over again it was *the sand in his shoes.*

The parallel of this story to marriage is striking. Most partners can tolerate the large mountain-like crises that confront every marriage from time to time. But it is those small irritants—including those pesky little criticisms— that erode the foundation of marriage. My husband and I both accuse each other of being a perfectionist. We habitually try to help each other improve, but our "help" is frequently perceived as criticism. To remind us to temper our perfectionistic tendencies, to eliminate the sand in our shoes, our daughter gave us a framed saying by Will Rogers:

> It's great to be great,
> but it's greater to be human.

To help put into practice Will Roger's wisdom, we have another framed saying hanging nearby:

> Keep your eyes wide open before marriage,
> half shut afterwards.

5. *Spend fallow time with each other.* Time together needs to be time that is not designated for work, demands of the children, housework, social obligations—or any other concern that diverts your attention from each other. A lot of couples say they spend time with each other, but it is time spent on everything but the marriage relationship. Shannon said this about her own situation:

> We are together a lot, but the agenda is always filled with social obligations, church meetings and lots of *good* activities. But Rick and I never have time just for us. I used to enjoy short car trips with Rick. We could talk for several hours with no interruptions. But now there's a telephone in the car . . . we're back where we started! I am ready to try what a friend suggested—asking Rick to "write me in" on his calendar.

The authors of "All Stressed Up and Someplace to Go" would probably agree with the friend's suggestion. They say that marriage partners need to build into their daily schedule "fallow times." They explain that fallow is a concept applied most often to land. In biblical times, farmers used a rotation system to revitalize their fields. For six years they would plant and harvest, but the seventh year the field was allowed to lie fallow. That year was a time to replenish and nourish.

A time out every seven years, of course, won't do the trick for marriage. Instead, we need time *daily* without any purpose or agenda other than simply taking time out to be with each other. Each couple will have to work out their own details as to how to put this concept into practice. To find fallow time, you no doubt will have to eliminate some other commitment or activity. The authors point out the benefits of your taking that step: "You may well find that your marriage responds like the lands of ancient Hebrews. The time off will rejuvenate and nurture the two of you and move you toward a more complete state of unity."[4]

6. *Enjoy the God-given sexual aspects of your marriage.* Any discussion of marriage without saying something about sex is like describing a hot bath with no mention of the delights of bubbles and scented oil. And just like other areas of marriage, sex can always get better. For starters, I suggest that you read *The Gift of Sex: A Christian Guide to Sexual Fulfillment* by Clifford and Joyce Penner. Read this book together, and put it into practice in your marriage. You will be glad you did!

Enjoyable sex is like the added splendor of an expensive fragrance. Special advice to husbands: Avoid being as harsh and hurried as a rough, hand-washed turkish towel. Special advise to wives: Avoid being as unenthusiastic as a sopping wet cloth left in the bottom of the tub after the dirty bath water has gurgled down the drain. Advice to both: Put less emphasis on *performance* and more on *pleasure.*

7. *Add lots of Living Water to your marriage.* Couples who receive God's gift of "living water" are less likely to find themselves in water over their heads. And if they do

experience problems, spiritual help sometimes can make the difference. It can save a marriage from going down the drain, or it can make a good one stronger and more satisfying. Take the case of Bob and Debbie Johns. Everyone who knows them agrees they are a dedicated couple. Not only do they *love* each other, they even *like* each other. They both say God has made the difference in their marriage. Bob explains:

> Marriage will be disappointing if you expect your marriage partner to fill all your needs for significance. Only since Debbie and I learned to put God first in our relationship have we been able to relax and love each other with a warm, accepting attitude.
>
> In my work with families, I have concluded that the ones who handle the stress and strains of daily living are those who, like Debbie and me, rely on God to help them love and accept and encourage each other.

Marriages may be made in heaven, but they have to be lived on earth so they need more than that initial romantic love to keep them warm and vibrant. Remember: Marriage is like a hot bath. Keep adding the warmth of a growing love, and it will last a lifetime.

MYTH 2:

The Key to a Happy Marriage Is Choosing the Right Mate

ONE OF THE MOST DANGEROUS myths about marriage is the assumption that finding the perfect partner can guarantee a happy marriage. The reality of the matter is this: Being the right kind of mate yourself is far more critical to your having a happy marriage than selecting a marriage partner with certain qualities. You and you alone are primarily responsible for your own happiness.

A Knight in Shining Armor

Ideally, your mate has your best interests at heart; unfortunately, though, this is not always the case. When you refuse to assume responsibility for your own contentment, you allow yourself to be terribly vulnerable. You become a pawn—or at least putty—in the hands of your mate; and all too often passivity in one mate brings out the worst in the other. For example, it might create in one spouse an urge to control or exert power over the other. Consider the comment of this disillusioned mate:

A knight in shining armor on a white horse is an elusive dream. When one does appear, he—or she—all too often is

10

looking for someone to follow along behind to do the dirty work.

One of my unmarried friends years ago made a statement I have remembered and thought about a lot: "I am looking for the ideal marriage partner. The only problem is that I'm afraid when I find her, she'll also be looking for the ideal mate." My friend's observation capsulized more truth than he probably ever realized.

People do need to consider that they may be judged by the same critical yardstick they use to evaluate others. The Scriptures remind us, ". . . in the way you judge, you will be judged; and by your standard of measure, it will be measured to you" (Matt. 7:2, NASB). Too often we judge ourselves by our ideal while we judge others by their actions. Consider for example, the following:

I offer *constructive criticism;* you are a *nag.*
I am *determined;* you are *stubborn.*
I am *tactful;* you are *apple polishing.*
I am *consistent;* you are *set in your ways.*
I *stand up* for what I believe; you are a *fanatic.*
I keep my things *organized;* you are a *compulsive neurotic.*
I use *discernment;* you are *picky.*
I am *careful about details;* you are a *fussbudget.*
I am *forthright;* you are a *loudmouth.*
I *take credit* where credit is due; you are a *braggart.*
I take *responsibility;* you are a *worrywart.*
I keep a *low profile;* you are a *wimp.*
I know how to *relax;* you are a *deadbeat.*
I look at things *realistically;* you are a *pessimist.*
I *don't take any guff* off anyone; you *pass the buck.*
I am *deliberate;* you are *dead slow.*
I am *accommodating;* you *compromise* your standards.
I *take advantage of opportunities;* you are a *vulture.*
ad nauseam

Taking Off the Mask

Here is an observation of great consequence: *Marriage will not change you greatly.* If, for example, you have a poor self-concept and are a sulky, insecure, selfish malcontent, then no matter whom you choose to marry, you will probably remain a sulky, insecure, selfish malcontent—hardly grounds for a happy marriage. One of my relatives with a knack for down-home wisdom expressed this same idea with an old, familiar saying: "You cannot make a silk purse out of a sow's ear." Another relative framed this notion with a little more sophistication: "Marriage does not change you, it merely unmasks you."

You can, of course, make dramatic changes in yourself; but it is a fallacy to expect marriage per se to make those changes. Self-understanding is the foundation for making needed changes. Jarrell learned this nugget of truth the hard—and almost fatal—way:

I was a driver. I worked hard and expected success in everything I did. I made no allowance for mistakes in myself or in others—especially my wife Wynn and our children. I expected Wynn to help me succeed in my career. "I'm doing this for you and the kids," I'd tell her when I pushed myself to the brink of mental and physical exhaustion. I was always "on guard" and uptight. As a result, Wynn and the kids constantly checked out my mood to make sure they didn't cross me. Wynn tiptoed around the house, fearful of making a wrong move. The kids usually just disappeared.

Speaking of the kids, I told Wynn they were mostly her responsibility. Of course, I didn't say that in words, but my actions said it loud and clear. I was always too busy to be bothered by them. I had important meetings to attend many evenings. When I was at home, I had a briefcase full of important papers to go through. I snapped orders to them like they were unfeeling robots.

The pressure at work and home built and finally exploded in a heart attack—a minor one, thank goodness, but major enough to get my attention. Lying in that hospital room, I had time to think about what was going on in my life. I took some long hard looks at myself, and I was disgusted with what I saw. I saw a selfish man who was scared to death— scared to death that my co-workers would find out I wasn't as great as I wanted them to think I was. Scared to death that

my wife would see me as a weakling. Scared to death I
would turn out to be a wimp like my father was. Scared to
death my kids would hate me like I hated my father. Scared
to death I would be a failure.

Realizing and recognizing the root cause of my unrealistic expectations was the beginning of understanding myself. I was so afraid of being an all-around failure. I wanted
deeply to be a success and to be happy. But I was going
about it all in a crazy way. My motives were all right but
my methods were all wrong. Understanding myself, why I
felt like I did and why I acted like I did, opened the door to
getting my life straightened out.

Shakespeare expressed the importance of self-understanding in *Hamlet:*

> This above all: to thine own self be true,
> And it must follow, as the night the day,
> Thou canst not then be false to any man.

Love Yourself

People who expect love from others and take it without
giving love in return are much like the Dead Sea. The Dead
Sea takes but never gives. As a result, its water is so stagnant and repugnant nothing can survive, much less grow in
it. A relationship with a person who only takes but never
gives also quickly turns sour.

But here is a paradox: People cannot give that which they
do not have. You must have love for yourself before you can
give it to another. "You must love others as much as yourself"
(Mark 12:31, TLB). The Bible clearly states that we are to love
others as much as ourselves—not *instead* of ourselves, and
not *more* than ourselves, but *as much as* ourselves.

Self-love and the ability to love someone else are closely
tied to self-respect and the ability to treat others with respect. The coin of respect, like that of love, has two sides.
One is respect for your own individuality, or your own selfhood. The other is respect for your marriage partner's individuality. Noted marriage expert Virginia Satir contends

that partners with self-love and self-respect enhance a relationship, for this kind of person "appreciates his own worth . . . [and] is ready to see and respect the worth of others."

Not a Fifty-Fifty Relationship

While each marriage partner should take responsibility for his or her own happiness, the familiar admonition that marriage should be a fifty-fifty proposition is only half right. The flourishing, fulfilling marriage relationship demands that *both* partners give 100 percent—that is, with both individuals assuming full responsibility for themselves and for their total commitment and effort to make the marriage work. The late columnist Sidney J. Harris once said:

> A marriage will flourish when it is composed of two persons who will nurse each other; it may even survive when one is a nurse and the other an invalid; but it is sure to collapse when it consists of two invalids, each needing a nurse."[1]

Don't make the mistake of assuming that the perfect marriage partner guarantees a happy marriage. Instead, the first prerequisite to a happy marriage is for you yourself to be a stable, secure, and sensible person willing and able to nourish and nurture another human being. Perhaps the best summation of what I am saying are the words of the great German philosopher Immanuel Kant:

> *It is God's will, not merely that we should be happy,*
> *but that we should make ourselves happy.*

MYTH 3:

Marriage Stifles Individuality

TWO PORCUPINES trying to stay warm on a cold winter's night provide a simple illustration of what happens in a healthy marriage. The two shivering creatures, desperate for warmth, are drawn together like two strong magnets. "Ouch!" they shriek in unison as their pointed, prickly quills pierce each other's tender skin. They quickly withdraw to alleviate the painful closeness. But they do not move as far away as they originally were. Then they cautiously creep toward each other a second time—only to jab each other again, but not quite so brutally as before. They jerk away from each other, then inch their way closer once more.

The two porcupines shift back and forth, experimenting anew to find a position providing the most warmth with the least discomfort. Once they find this strategic location in relationship to each other, they enjoy a secure, peaceful respite from the world's blustery and wintery winds. Their quills are still sharp; the meshing together doesn't weaken them. But the animals have found a way to be themselves, while enjoying being close to one another. Rested, restored, and rejuvenated, they are ready to brave the cold, cruel world the next day.

Perhaps fictitious, this story of two porcupines nevertheless paints a clear mental picture of what takes place
in marriage as each spouse expresses his or her individuality. Marriage experts give this dilemma various labels,
including "separateness and connectedness," "distance reg-
ulation," "separateness and belongingness," and "differen-
tiation and integration." Whatever the terms, the challenge
is the same. In marriage, two people attempt the paradoxical task of coming together while staying apart. To enjoy
the generative warmth of a close relationship, people—like
porcupines—simply have to learn to mesh their individual
traits with those of their spouse.

Two Are Better Than One

The ideal relationship, however, provides more satisfaction than sacrifice. Human beings derive their meaning
from others, from relationships. Humans are by nature
social; they are beings created for communication with others. Their "source of creativity," says Hazen G. Werner in
The Bible and the Family, "is found . . . with other persons." As a member of a group that scaled Mount Everest
observed, "No one climbs alone."
    The Bible itself reports God saying in the beginning of
all creation, "It is not good that the man should be alone"
(Gen. 2:18, KJV). Solomon, considered one of the wisest men
of all times, said, "Two are better than one," (Eccles. 4:9,
KJV), and he added that if one falls, the other can lift that
one up (Eccles. 4:10).
    Anne Morrow Lindbergh captures the essence of a nour-
ishing marriage relationship in this beautiful description:

A good relationship has a pattern like a dance and is built
on some of the same rules. The partners do not need to hold
on tightly because they move confidently in the same pattern, intricate, swift, and free, like a country dance of
Mozart's. There is no place here for the possessive clutch,
the clinging arm, the heavy hand; only the barest touch in
passing. Now arm in arm, now face to face, now back to

back—it does not matter which. Because they know they are partners moving to the same rhythm, creating a pattern together, and being invisibly nourished by it.[1]

Using Marriage as an Excuse

Some people attack marriage, saying it is a trap, a dismal prison in which unsuspecting people find themselves locked. Popular quips reflect a freedom-robbing mindset:
"He has lost his freedom."
"He's giving up. . . ."
"He finally trapped her."
One disconsolate soul claimed, "Marriage offers love but then engenders hate. It promises the unfolding of the personality but actually stultifies happiness and delivers wretched misery." That there have been and are such miserable marriages, the experts readily admit. But marriage is not necessarily like this; nor does it have to be. Those who contend that marriage is a restrictive cage need to check the cage door. It may not be locked. In fact, it might swing open with one gentle push. Dean, a successful businessman and husband, shares this insight:

> Many persons like to hide behind their assertion that marriage has failed, whereas in reality they, as individuals, have failed to make the most of what marriage has to offer.

People who say marriage confines them and denies them freedom of expression probably would be inexpressive and inept as single individuals as well. Some people need an excuse for their own personal inertia, lack of motivation, shortcomings, and failure to achieve their life goals. Marriage can easily become their scapegoat.

Couples who are able to handle the requirements of marriage contend that the tradeoffs and delights make all the demands worthwhile. Wayne, a highly respected school administrator, a dependable church worker, and a devoted husband and father of two teenagers, concludes: "Sure, marriage and parenting take a lot of time and energy, but

the fringe benefits are *greater* forces of creativity and freedom, not *less.* "

Increased Freedom of Choice

But let's back up a moment and consider the decision of
whether to get married in the first place. Because of changing cultural and social attitudes, we enjoy more freedom of
choice about this matter than ever before.

This freedom to marry or not to marry allows individuals to choose which lifestyle they believe will provide them
the most happiness. That happiness often is measured by
opportunity to express themselves and to develop their individuality. Even the marriage experts admit there are
probably some people who should *not* marry; they would
be happier unmarried because their goals and their personalities may be better suited to single life. On the other
hand, there are some whose personalities and temperaments suit them for the sharing and give-and-take that
marriage requires.

We are also freer than ever before to marry whomever
we want to marry. Social and religious restrictions are more
lenient than they have ever been in human history. In addition, we are freer than ever before to create the marriage
style that suits our needs, personality, and preferences. So,
marriage offers more freedom than ever before. With increased and varied options, people should be able to choose
those which provide the most opportunities for their own
unique individual expression and development.

Creating a Masterpiece Marriage

What is a "masterpiece" marriage? What kind of marriage provides for freedom of expression and development
of individuality? No hard-and-fast answer can be offered,
for what "works" for one couple does not work for another.
The key lies in the agreement the two marriage partners
can work out about the kind of marriage they each want
and the willingness of each to do what it takes to create
that marriage.

One couple who had the reputation for having a master-piece marriage had informally counseled numerous other couples during their own thirty-year marriage. When I asked them what formula they used for their own vivacious relationship, Kent quickly responded, "Oh, it's easy. We just use the magic Seven Cs formula!" That sounded so roman-tic, I asked for an explanation. Kent and his wife Elaine replied almost in unison, "Converse, combat, concede, com-ply, compromise, conciliate, and compliment."

Both Kent and Elaine are strong, expressive individuals. Without their strength of individuality, Elaine says, it might not have been possible for them to think so positively about their togetherness. Individuality might be defined as inde-pendence of thought, feeling, and judgment. It includes a firm sense of autonomy, personal responsibility, identity, and boundaries of self. In contrast, togetherness, or mutual-ity, refers to a sense of emotional closeness, joining, or inti-macy. The twin notions of *individuality* and *mutuality* are inextricably wed. Paradoxically, healthy mutuality occurs only when the two partners have a strong, healthy sense of individuality. Otherwise, they may feel smothered by the marriage. With their strong individuality, Kent and Elaine seem to have mastered the art of investing themselves in their relationship without losing their sense of self in the process.

Another couple I know has a strong marriage, but it is quite different from the "Seven Cs" couple. Daryl and Gwen have what some experts call a "utilitarian" marriage. They tend to view their marriage as a mutually advanta-geous merger, but they actually gratify many of their needs for expression and development outside the marital rela-tionship. "I saw early in our marriage," Gwen points out, "that Daryl loved his job and was going to spend a lot of time and energy climbing the career ladder. So I found an enjoyable outlet in worthwhile community programs and in my church."

Some women would have failed to take Gwen's positive approach; they might have stayed home sulking alone, fail-ing to develop their individuality while the husband busied himself with his career. Adds Gwen, "We have a good marriage. The time we spend together is happy. And our different activities and interests enrich our relationship."

The emphasis in the last few decades on equality, individual rights, freedom, self-awareness, personal growth, self-realization, and self-actualization seems to map out the road to happiness via the route of self-centered, "me-first" psychology. Many unwittingly hold onto the misconception that meeting the needs of our marriage partner necessitates sacrificing our own freedom and individuality. Yet convincing evidence indicates that seeking self-gratification has not delivered the expected happiness nor the freedom for self-expression. Instead, a generous portion of "otherness," rather than an all-absorbing "selfness," contributes to emotional well-being as well as to the development of individuality.

A marriage in which both partners work hard at developing individuality and mutuality forms the warp and the woof of an interdependence that enables the individual and the marriage to flourish. The sense of belonging, the sense of being needed, and the sense of mutual support that marriage provides may empower a wellspring of creativity and individual development. "What creates in one the consciousness of being a person," pointed out the eminent Swiss psychiatrist Dr. Paul Tournier, "is entering into a relationship with another person."[2]

The scripture that states, "Two can accomplish more than twice as much as one," (Eccles. 4:9, TLB) continues with these words from which an implicit analogy to the marriage relationship might be made: "Also, on a cold night, two under the same blanket gain warmth from each other, but how can one be warm alone?" (Eccles. 9:11, TLB). Or to put it more simply, marriage does not automatically restrict the freedom of individuals to express themselves and to develop their individuality. In fact, many of the most creative, fulfilled individuals are those in marriages in which the partners feel a sense of responsibility for self *and* the other, and search for ways to provide the maximum satisfaction with the minimum discomfort. Just like two porcupines on a cold winter's night.

MYTH 4:

Spouses Must Be Compatible

COMPATIBILITY—that vague, indefinite term we use to label the ability of two marriage partners to live together in harmony—has fascinated family experts for years. In fact, the notion of compatibility was first recorded by Plato over 2,000 years ago. But this age-old idea that a husband and wife must fit each other like pieces of a jigsaw puzzle is just a myth, as shown by the undue grief it has caused countless couples down through the years. When couples expect to be in total agreement on everything, they set themselves up for failure.

Experts and completely honest couples admit that every successful marriage demands time-consuming adjusting, adapting, cooperating, compromising—and occasionally arguing—throughout the marriage. I am reminded of an observation Billy Graham once made on television. He said when a mate brags of a forty- or fifty-year marriage with no arguments, "either that marriage partner is lying, or one of the partners is unnecessary."

All or Nothing

A misconception about compatibility is running amuck right now. It's the "all-or-nothing" notion. In other words, either you *are* compatible or you *are not.* In reality, though, a couple may be compatible in some areas but have difficulty working out an agreeable approach to handling other areas of their marriage. Don and Jan, a couple with over twenty years of marital combat and cohesion under their belts, are a good illustration. Here is what Jan has to say:

> Don and I pretty well agree on how to spend our money. We enjoy our church activities together. Our sex life is good. But deciding how to use our free time brings out the worst in us. Don likes to watch television and go hunting with the guys. I'd like for us to spend more time doing things together around the house and go on short trips together. We get along well with our daughters, but we have some heated differences on how to relate to our son.

Don explains how he and Jan handle their incompatibilities:

> We accept the fact that no two human beings can live together without occasional differences of opinion. Even though we are alike in many ways, we are almost opposite in others. Early in our marriage—after some awful arguments that got us nowhere—we agreed to follow certain ground rules for working out decisions we both can live with. A basic rule is that we always treat each other with respect—which is really hard to do when we each think our own way of thinking or doing is absolutely the better or smarter way. And we have made a commitment to each other to always *fight fair.*

Jan agrees that her marriage to Don consists of some compatible areas but also some areas that require a little more compromise. She adds:

> No two people could be completely compatible—that's humanly impossible. Only clones would hold the exact same attitudes and opinions. And how boring that would be!

Once and for All

One of the most troublesome myths in my own marriage is the expectation that once my husband and I come to an agreement on some issue or some vital area of our relationship, that it is then settled *once and for all.* Rarely is this the case. It is not that my husband and I change our minds; it is that not just one but often two or three or more significant factors change in the situation. Such changes within a marriage relationship constantly alter the complexion of compatibility. And while it's helpful to establish constructive ways of communicating and coping with these changes early in marriage, I have observed that some of the most challenging adjustments actually come later in the relationship. If the once-and-for-all illusion is not completely exploded during the early stage of marriage, it probably will be later on.

I for one was certainly not expecting this. Ever since I can remember thinking about marriage, I can recall being reminded what a big adjustment marriage would demand. Maybe in the early days I was so blinded by infatuation I didn't notice these adjustments, or maybe the honeymoon glow glossed over any drastic accommodations. Later, however, I found that adding a third member to our couple status demanded much more adapting than I had experienced by simply getting married. A baby requires attention around the clock; a marriage partner allows a few hours latitude now and then.

Several of my friends shared a similar experience. And adding another baby to a household already ravaged by a child in the "Terrible Two" stage generally threatens the best of marital harmony. The tumultuous teen-age years also are known to jeopardize the compatibility and tranquillity of many couples. Then when one or both marriage partners are smitten by a bad case of the middle-age crazies, the marital boat is rocked still more.

Aging parents needing extra attention create extreme distress and divisiveness for many couples. Retirement of one or both marriage partners—usually anticipated with eagerness—requires more adjustments than many couples realize. Add economic problems (sometimes unemployment) to these so-called "normal" adjustments or pressures, and the unity and compatibility of many marriages is out the back door, at least until the couple can work out constructive

ways to deal with the pressure points—or until the pressure
passes.

To further complicate the compatibility mystery, qualities
which contribute to compatibility at one stage of a relationship may not be the same traits or characteristics that enhance the relationship at a different stage. Phil and Nancy,
for example, found their harmony disrupted when their child
was grown. Phil is a quiet, steady introvert while Nancy is a
bubbly, impulsive extrovert. But these differences were not
bothersome during the early years of their marriage.

Phil explains: "We were simply too busy with our baby
to clash with each other in the early years of marriage. . . .
Differences in our personalities surprisingly surfaced as
flaws in the tapestry of our marital harmony after we both
were established in our careers and our one child went away
to college."

Nancy wanted to go and see places and be with friends
after those years of rearing their daughter and getting
started in her "other" career. Phil, on the other hand, wanted
to stay home and relax after those hectic childrearing days
and demanding years of working his way up in the company. But they learned the value of compromise as Phil
agreed to join Nancy in a local square dance club and to eat
out occasionally. Nancy was satisfied to spend some
evenings at home and have friends over now and then to eat
or watch a special television program.

Unlike many other couples, Phil and Nancy luckily became aware of their mistaken notion about compatibility.
They recognized that to maintain any degree of compatibility, married partners simply must view marriage as a
never-ending adjustment to myriad changes rather than an
all-or-nothing or a once-and-for-all proposition.

Complementary Needs

A longstanding theory maintains that compatible marriages are more probable if mates select each other on the
basis of how they complement each other. The common
definition of the word *complement* sums up the essence of

this theory. It means "to round out, to complete, or to bring to perfection." A literal application of this viewpoint suggests that a person who likes to dominate, for example, should marry someone who likes to be dominated. Someone who is indecisive should marry someone who is forceful and makes decisions easily and quickly. A spendthrift should marry someone with opposite inclinations to "complement" or balance out his or her habits. A messy person should marry a neat person, and so on.

While this complementary-needs notion may explain harmony or compatibility in some couples some of the time in some of the areas of their relationship, it fails to explain disparaging marital murmurs like these:

> "His throwing his things around the house drives me crazy."
> "She thinks money grows on trees."
> "I wish she could make at least one decision on her own."
> "Who does he think he is, bossing me around all the time?"

Subconscious Needs

We are aware of some of the needs we expect marriage to meet, such as the desire for companionship, for sex, or for the status of being married, but many of our needs are subconscious. These subliminal forces can play havoc with marital harmony when we are not aware of what is motivating our actions or feelings. This is especially true because some of our needs are irrational—if not outright neurotic. Take the wife, for example, who insists to her husband, "Of course, I don't care if you watch the Sunday afternoon football game and Monday night football." Then she works feverishly cleaning house, glaring at her husband and seething as he relaxes on the sofa and watches the game. Hostility builds up in her, satisfying her unconscious need to feel like a martyr.

Or consider the husband who constantly complains about his wife's housekeeping regardless of how conscientiously she tries to comply with his suggestions. He may be suffering from feelings of incompetence in his own role of chief breadwinner, so subconsciously he struggles to build up his waning ego by criticizing his wife with putdowns about what he defines as her role as housekeeper.

Three Cheers for Incompatibility!

One person's medicine is another's poison. This old folk saying may apply especially to compatibility, for we have all seen marriages which have many of the trappings of harmony, yet provoke our thoughts of, *Boy, I'd hate to be married to him,* or *How in the world does he put up with her?*

Another similar saying expresses the experience of countless couples: "The shoe that fits one person pinches the other." Happily married couples are those who are able to work out a pattern or style of marriage that suits them best. While some couples seem to thrive on conflict, others are devastated by it. Some couples are happy working closely together as much as possible, while others simply cannot tolerate a constant dose of companionship.

One wife who contends that she and her husband of twenty-seven years are "very happy" says, "We like each other better and we have a happier marriage when we don't spend every waking minute together. Too much togetherness is not for us."

A friend of Ruth Graham evidently felt the same way. Mrs. Graham, wife of the famous Billy Graham, shared that she and two friends were having lunch one day while their husbands were playing golf. The older companion asked a tantalizing question something like this: "Want to know the secret of our happy marriage?" Mrs. Graham reported that with forks in midair, she and the other friend waited to hear what the woman would say. The friend's eyes sparkled mischievously as she said, "We never do anything together . . . except sleep together."

Mrs. Graham said the three were still chuckling when their husbands joined them. "Her words ringing in my ears," Mrs. Graham commented, "I noticed the affectionate kiss her husband gave her." Mrs. Graham concluded, "All I can say is 'Three cheers for incompatibility!'"[1]

In the thought-provoking book *Incompatibility: Grounds for a Great Marriage!*, an analogy is given illustrating the diversity that can exist in unity and strength. When cars were first invented, steel tires were used on them. These cast-iron circles withstood whatever punishment the unpaved, rocky roads meted out. But the poor passengers endured some pretty rough traveling. Later, rubber tires were developed; they provided a smoother ride but seemed to wear away like melting butter. Finally, someone came up with the brilliant idea of wedding the steel's toughness with the rubber's ability to give a smoother ride. When marriage partners make a commitment to weld their differences into a strong marriage, they can indeed create a marriage strong enough to endure the bumps and bruises of life yet resilient enough to absorb the jolts and provide a pleasant journey.[2]

A romanticist might say a happy marriage is like an instrument of many strings. Each couple must work at blending the diverse aspects of their marriage to find the harmony and melody that is most pleasing to them.

A chemist might say that the marriage of two personalities is like the contact of two dissimilar chemical substances: If there is any reaction, both are transformed.

Being neither a romanticist nor a chemist, but a pragmatic realist, I would say that the best marriage is simply a polite agreement of two people to put up with each other's seemingly intolerable ways.

The acceptance of these qualifications for a good marriage shatters the damaging myth that to be happily married, spouses have to be compatible. Human experience shows that when marriage partners expect every little edge and shape of their relationship to fit together like the interlocking pieces of a jigsaw puzzle, they are setting themselves up for disappointment. In contrast, those who shed this romantic fantasy about compatibility can live out the ageless truth that in diversity there can be strength and unity, and they can say merrily along with Mrs. Graham:

Three cheers for incompatibility!

MYTH 5:

Marriage Partners Need to Look for Weaknesses in Their Marriage and Fix Them

THE STORY IS TOLD of a young child who did not talk until he was five years old. The parents worried themselves sick, taking him to numerous specialists trying to find out why he did not say anything. Then one morning he was sitting at the breakfast table when his mother put some dark toast on his plate in front of him. He glanced down at the toast, looked up at his mother, and said clearly and distinctly, "This toast is burned!"

The mother was ecstatic. After she revived from the shock of that momentous outburst of language, she asked her young son, "Since you can talk so well, why in the world haven't you talked before now?"

"Well," he explained deliberately, "everything was all right up until now."

Amusing as this story may be, unfortunately, it reminds me of marriages in which partners speak to each other mostly when something is wrong. They rarely say anything complimentary to each other. They have fallen prey to the myth that marriage partners need to concentrate on weaknesses in their marriage so they can eliminate them. Or they may simply have fallen into the discouraging habit of dwelling on the negative, with no particular intention or desire to make improvements. Whatever their motive, they fail to realize that the most satisfying marriages are built on the strengths of the two mates, not on preoccupation with their weaknesses.

Accentuate the Positive

The Law of Emotional Gravity says that one pessimist can pull down five optimists easier than five optimists can lift up one pessimist. Albert Einstein, best known for his theory of relativity, deserves recognition for yet another feat: He and his wife were happily married for over sixty years. He applied the same scientific approach to marriage that he did to experiments in his laboratory. About this notion of negativity in the marriage relationship, he once observed: "One incorrect input requires eleven correct inputs to make things right again." Einstein recognized and lived by the premise that individuals who enjoy fulfilling marriages are propelled by thoughts of their best hours, their greatest optimism, and their most triumphant experiences.

In contrast, persons suffering dull, downcast, or dour marriages are often controlled by past mistakes, disappointments, and defeats. Concentrating on these negatives does not accomplish anything. Instead, it is discouraging and counterproductive, insidiously gnawing away at marital harmony. The book *Making Things Right When Things Go Wrong* includes a chapter called "Cut Your Line When It's Tangled," offering marriage counselor Paul Faulkner's graphic description of how marriage partners waste a lot of today's time and energy trying to straighten out yesterday's problems. He suggests, figuratively speaking, "Why not cut the line and get back to fishing?" He then draws his analogy to the old-fashioned slop bucket:

When you were a kid, did your mom or grandma have a slop bucket? You know, it sat over in some out-of-sight corner in the old kitchen where the smell couldn't be detected too easily. Sometimes it even had a lid. And every few minutes when she was cooking Grandma would throw something in there that she didn't want to keep—trimmings off the meat, potato peels, spoiled milk and all the rest of the leftover food garbage. I think "slop" was a good name for it.

Then about every two or three days someone would have to take that bucket full of slop and go pour it into the pig's trough. Sometimes that old pig would get so excited about eating he couldn't wait for them to finish pouring, and he'd stick his head under the pouring slop. Well, I've found out that folks carry their own personal slop buckets around with them. Especially married folks do. But these are emotional slop buckets. We fill them up with all our leftover feelings and emotions from spats and quarrels. We throw in the trimmings from old conflicts and disagreements. We just collect all sorts of emotional slop from our past.

Then, every so often, when our emotions are running high over some current problem, we grab up our slop buckets and empty them on the heads of our husband, wife, kids or friends. We pour out all the slop from our past and muck up the present with it. It's disgusting![1]

In striking contrast, a serene and satisfying union flourishes best when partners emphasize the present golden strengths of each other and of the marriage itself.

Practice Being Positive!

Recognizing the folly of concentrating on weaknesses is a vital step toward dispelling the harmful effects of this myth. It is not enough, however, to simply *think positively;* you must diligently put into practice concrete steps to *act positively.* It will not come naturally; you must work at it. Drilling yourself to try to establish the habit of being positive produces results, just as Galatians 6:7 says: Whatever we sow, we will also reap. Case in point: Dr. Robert Schuller and his wife have been married about forty years.

He says, "One of the reasons we are closer than ever is that we train ourselves to be sensitive to negative experiences and input, and we don't let them get to us."

Dr. Schuller relates a story he read about a gigantic tree in Colorado that blew down. The tree was nearly 500 years old; it was a sapling when Columbus landed on American shores. Lightning had struck the huge tree fourteen times, but it had survived. Not only had it survived lightning, it had defied the ravages of freezing snow and ice and even the destructive force of an earthquake. What destroyed this apparently immortal tree? Some tiny beetles bore their way first through the bark and then to the core of the tree.[2]

Negative thoughts and comments, like those tiny beetles, may not seem like much of a threat, but they can pierce the outer protective layer of individuals, attacking the innermost psyche and selfhood and inflicting the deepest hurt, and destroying the warm, caring feelings and the trust that furnish the lifeblood of the marriage relationship. Make a commitment to each other today to practice keeping negativity out of your relationship!

But being positive involves more than simply *not* being negative. It requires an uplifting attitude and affirming comments to each other. A story about a married couple celebrating their twenty-fifth wedding anniversary illustrates this point well. The husband came in from work and found his wife crying her eyes out. He asked, "What in the world is wrong?"

"Today is our silver anniversary," she sobbed, "and I can remember only one time your telling me you loved me and that was nearly twenty-five years ago." While she continued to weep, the husband—a kind soul who had rarely said anything negative the entire twenty-five years of marriage—stroked his chin with a faraway look in his eyes, thinking back to the time when he had spoken those words to her. Turning and looking directly at her, he said matter-of-factly, "I can remember telling you that I loved you . . . and if I change my mind, I'll let you know."

To fill the marriage with good will and to build bonds of affection, eliminate the negative, but also *practice being positive!* When spirits droop or when you are tempted to be negative, apply the psychology as expressed in Proverbs 12:25: "Anxious hearts are very heavy but a word of encouragement does wonders!" (TLB).

Keep Things in Perspective

One of my friends admits he is a reformed perfectionist. Early in his marriage his reaction was always volatile about anything that was not quite right. He explains, "Long months spent away from my family in my twenty-plus years in the military, including combat in Vietnam, made me realize the value of perspective in all things, and especially in marriage." He continues, "Of course, you need a balance . . . some things are serious and deserve your attention and correction. But for the sake of my marriage, I wish I had learned sooner not to make mountains out of molehills."

Another reformed perfectionist, "a former nagger," as she put it, offers a similar Road-to-Damascus experience:

I grew up in a house that was always in shambles. I was even embarrassed to bring friends home with me. My dream for marriage was to have a spotless home, always neat and polished—a shining showcase! My husband grew up in that very kind of home. And he detested it. His dream house was a comfortable, homey place where he could relax, let down, and catch as catch can. Our visions of a dreamland marriage shattered soon after the honeymoon. Our fantasies turned into a nightmare as our diametrically opposed notions about marriage clashed day in and day out.

The situation worsened when our children got older because we both tried to impose our standards on them. Since our standards were so different, our children were caught in the crossfire, never quite certain what to do. The only thing they were sure of was that they knew they could never please both of us at the same time.

I can't quite recall any specific event that finally made me realize that my expectations were not creating the "happy little home" that I had longed for. My intentions were good, but my method simply didn't work. I wish I

could say the changes were made as quickly and easily as
my realization that some changes had to be made. Not so.
But when I confessed to my husband that I was willing
to lay down the whip, he immediately agreed to do more to
accommodate my need for neatness and adherence to the
creeds, "A place for everything and everything in its place"
and "Cleanliness is next to Godliness."

Our marriage became a lot happier when we started
trying to keep things in perspective.

Let Bygones Be Bygones

Late in the second quarter of the 1929 Rose Bowl game,
Georgia Tech fumbled the football on its own thirty-three
yard line. The California center, Roy Riegels, scooped up
the ball, spun around, and raced toward the goal line. Seconds before he reached the end zone, one of his own team-
mates tackled him. Roy Riegels had run sixty-seven yards
the wrong way! Humiliated by his mistake, Roy buried his
face in his hands in the locker room at halftime. The coach
spoke no words of reproach. When it was time to go out for
the second half, he simply said, "The same players who
started will begin the second half."

Roy did not budge. "Please Coach," he begged, "don't ask
me to go back out there after what I've done."

The coach put his hand on Roy's shoulder. "Let's go, Roy.
The game is only half over."

Roy returned to the field and played with more iron-
willed determination than any of the other players.[3]

We all make mistakes in marriage. We sometimes race off
the wrong way. Our attitude and actions are at times misguided and misdirected. We do dumb things. We say stupid,
thoughtless words. We feel like giving up. We may need
a wise mate who, like Roy Riegels's coach, tells us, "Let's
go . . . the game is only half over." Our mates may desper-
ately need to hear us say these comforting confidence-
building words.

Marriages that not only survive but thrive are those in
which both partners serve as encouraging coaches to each

other. They refuse to let ghosts from the past continually haunt their marriage, digging in to scars from past wounds and stirring up old bitterness anew. They refuse to give in to the human temptation to return evil for evil. They agree with the philosophy Paul Faulkner so colorfully expresses in *Making Things Right When Things Go Wrong:*

> Trying to get even is like trying to win a puking contest with a buzzard. He's a professional! And you simply can't win playing his game.

Partners who enjoy the best marriage are those who overlook mistakes. They forgive and forget. They take seriously Colossians 3:13 (TLB): "Be gentle and ready to forgive; never hold grudges. Remember, the Lord forgave you, so you must forgive others."

One wife once remarked to me, "I can forgive, but I have a hard time forgetting." Her comment reflects a misunderstanding that many of us hold. The key word is *forgetting.* In this case, it does not mean *not remembering.* Few of us can absolutely wipe away recollections from the past. Forgetting, in this sense, simply means "no longer being affected or influenced by something." It means "stop living in the past!" Or, to put it more concisely, "Let bygones be bygones."

Use the Act-As-If Principle

Maybe you are thinking, *I don't feel like being positive,* or *emphasizing the strengths in my marriage just doesn't seem natural.* Then you need to use the Act-As-If principle. William James, father of American psychology, said if you want to cultivate a desired attitude or habit, you can do it by acting as if you already have it. James maintained that the greatest discovery is realizing that by changing the inner attitudes of their minds human beings can change all the outer aspects of their lives. If you are a negative person, for example, but you want to be positive, *act* positively. If you persist in acting as if you are positive, you will ultimately become positive.

The Act-As-If principle has proved effective for many successful people. Before Liberace became famous as a concert pianist, for instance, he would put on his very best concert clothes and go to a renowned recital hall which he had rented. There he would play the piano as if he were performing a prestigious concert to a packed concert hall. The Act-As-If principle worked for Liberace, and it will work for you.

Experts on depression, psychiatrists Frank B. Minirth and Paul D. Meier wrote in their book *Happiness Is a Choice* that *behavior* changes *attitudes,* and not the other way around. O. H. Mowrer made a similar statement: "It is easier to act yourself into a better way of feeling than to feel yourself into a better way of acting." And Dr. George Crane said, "If you go through the *motion,* you'll feel the *emotion.*"

Is it deceptive to act a way you do not feel? Are you compromising your personal integrity if you act optimistic while in your heart of hearts you feel like the world's lowest pessimist? Doesn't the Act-As-If principle contradict all the advice about being genuine, transparent, and authentic, getting in touch with your real, gut-level feelings, and being honest with yourself and others? Not at all! Trying to be your very best self by striving to incorporate more positive qualities into your natural behavior is a noble motive. You are not a hypocrite unless you are simply pretending in order to mislead others, or you are "putting on an act" to manipulate your mate or others and never intend to make these qualities your very own.

The motto, "Fake it 'til you make it," is used by members of Alcoholics Anonymous to encourage each other one day at a time not to drink. Their motive is certainly genuine, and since their approach seems to work better than any other, I think it deserves serious consideration in other areas of behavior we wish to change for the better—like being more positive in our marriage and concentrating on strengths instead of weaknesses.

You may be thinking to yourself, *All this sounds easy in theory but what person can do it?* The Bible has an answer to your question: "Humanly speaking, no one. But with God, everything is possible" (Matt. 19:26, TLB). When you ask God to empower you and you enthusiastically Act-As-If your prayer is being answered, you will experience a striking change, not only in your actions but in your attitude. The word *enthusiasm,* in fact, is made up of two parts. The *en* means "in," and the rest of the word comes from *theos,* which means "God." So the word *enthusiasm* literally means "God in you." The rewards of this approach are immeasurable. When you begin to act upon the belief that it's your attitude that determines your happiness and not your circumstances, your marriage will soon reflect that truth.

What to Change and What to Overlook

Let's face it. Our marriage partners do not always please us. In fact, some of their habits or mannerisms drive us wild. While we should avoid dwelling on these faults and foibles, denying their existence is akin to ostriches foolishly hiding their heads in the sand. Our thinking may be guided by Reinhold Niebuhr's famous prayer distributed by the millions to military personnel during World War II, printed on greeting cards the world over, and adopted as the motto of Alcoholics Anonymous:

O God, give us serenity to accept what cannot be changed, courage to change what should be changed, and wisdom to distinguish one from the other.

"Courage to change what should be changed" would, in my expectations for marriage, apply to excessive drinking, abuse, financial irresponsibility, and unfaithfulness. I would seek professional help for any of these. Your list might be different. Marriage partners must decide for themselves what they want out of marriage. They must then distinguish between the blemishes they can tolerate, and the character flaws and failings so serious they hack away even at a Rock-of-Gibralter marriage.

After all is said and done, it is best to remember that the most satisfying marriages are those in which the two partners emphasize the strengths of each other and minimize the weaknesses. Marital partners might well profit from the practical advice William James recorded in an 1890 book called *The Principles of Psychology:*

> *The art of being wise is the art of knowing what to overlook.*

MYTH 6:

Variety Is the Spice of Life and of Marriage

WHILE IT IS TRUE that *boredom* may sound the death knell for romance, most areas of marriage are simply not enhanced by a *variety* of habits and beliefs. The gears of marital harmony can be gummed up by variations in ways of thinking and doing that range from the ridiculous to the sublime—but all too often top-heavy on the ridiculous.

For example, variety in habits may seem trivial or insignificant—until they make their abrupt and startling debut on the marital stage. Consider how warm affection turns to icicles when two players clash on a "little thing" like which way the toilet paper hangs, or the toothpaste tube is squeezed. Temperature is another place where variety can wreak havoc. I know two couples who spend most of their waking hours adjusting thermostats or confabbing about temperatures in general. In each case, one mate is hot-natured, the other cold-natured. One likes everything hot, the other prefers things cold. Rooms, coffee, food, soup, bed coverings—everything is either too hot, or too cold for these spouses.

Another instance of variety going against the grain of
marriage partners is in timing. This one difference alone
can put light years between husband-and-wife unity. Within our circle of acquaintances, I know of several marriages
in which one partner has a keen sense of time and insists on
living life like clockwork, arriving everywhere right on the
minute, while the other mate never gets anywhere on time
nor does anything according to a timetable. Imagine the
potential for conflict when fifteen minutes inevitably turns
out to be more like thirty.

The tendency these days seems to blame the failure of
marriage on wrong choice of mate, on poor communication,
or on simply "growing apart." To be sure, such matters are
frequently factors in the picture—but not always the most
divisive ones. In case after case with which I am familiar, the
underlying cause of marital breakdown is conflicts or clashes
over differences between the two marriage partners. For
many, variety simply does not provide the kind of spice that
brews a satisfying marriage. Throughout the remainder of
this chapter we'll look at some of the most significant aspects of marriage in which differences foster ill will.

Variety in Values

Values are sort of like the air we breathe. We do not see
air; we take it for granted. But it serves an essential function. Air gives us life and vitality, energy and force. Likewise, we cannot "see" values, but the values two people
hold—those deep-seated beliefs about people, things, and
ideas—exert powerful and pervasive impact on the quality
of their relationship. And similarity of values, not variety,
seems to foster more positive feelings.

I saw a bumper sticker several years ago that made a
good point. It's simply this:

USE THINGS, NOT PEOPLE

Whether we live by the value expressed in this bumper
sticker or not comes out loud and clear in the marriage

relationship. Case in point: Rita's husband Carl placed little value on human dignity and the worth of the individual—especially his wife. If you asked him pointblank, he would deny it, of course, but the proof of the pudding was in his attitudes and actions. That is the way values are. People may say they believe a certain way, but their *actions*, not their *words*, are a more accurate indicator of what they actually believe.

Carl was insecure, and his attitude and actions were ones of suspicion, judgment, and faultfinding. He was a self-appointed critic of everyone, and he consistently sharpened his critic's claws on Rita, always justifying his hurtful critiques with comments like these:

"I just want to help you."

"This is for your own good."

"I'm just telling you so you won't make the same mistake next time."

"I thought you would want to know what you've done wrong."

Carl genuinely thought it was his God-given right and responsibility to set Rita straight. He was sure that his opinions were far superior to those of everybody else.

Rita, on the other hand, longed to be treated with the same dignity and respect with which she treated others. Unfortunately, the extreme differences in Carl's and Rita's attitudes led to a marriage wrought with anger, resentment, fear, hostility, and eventually divorce—rather than one of comfort, trust, and acceptance.

Variety of opinion about money may also cause conflict within the marriage. To be painfully personal, my husband and I, for example, struggled long and hard in the early years of our marriage because of a simple difference in our beliefs on the nature of money. I think money is to *spend*, and my husband thinks it is to *save*. I grew up in a situation where "enough" money was not a problem; if I spent what I had, I generally could get more. My husband's background was quite different. With seven children in his family, when each spent the allotted amount, there was no more. It was as simple as that.

With a little imagination you can see the problems these different philosophies could create for a young couple struggling on an early-marriage income. Deep, searching conversations—and checkbook balancing—prodded us to realize that variety was *not* the spice of life in the case of our diametrically different beliefs about money.

Another money-value problem area has to do with how you view "things" in your life. A person may have grown up with the notion—perhaps out of necessity—that you should "use it up," "wear it out," or "make do." This mate's wants and wishes for the family income and how to spend it—or *not* spend it—will create discord and disagreements with the ideas of a mate who acts as though the house and everything in it are expendable.

Variety in Goals

A number of years ago when I was in Western Africa, my co-workers and I were assigned a guide. This weathered old man, recommended as one of the most experienced and best, said to us, "You have to agree where you are going. Then I can figure out how to get there." This practical wisdom applies equally as well to marriage. Unfortunately, however, a lot of couples have not decided on a destination for their marriage, so how in the world can they figure out how to get there?

Many marriage partners may have their own goals in mind, but they are not well crystallized—much less shared with their partner. And many may think or even say their goals are such and such—but their behavior indicates quite different goals. For instance, Becky said she wanted to be a good wife and mother, but she spent most of her time doing volunteer work, socializing with wives of her husband's professional colleagues, and working out at the health club. Consider her analysis:

> My husband and I attended an all-day family enrichment session, and it was an eye-opener for both of us. We realized

that it was no wonder our marriage seemed to lack direction and purpose. We had never really talked about what we wanted out of marriage and certainly not how to work at attaining that goal.

Talking about what we wanted from our marriage helped us formulate specific plans for reaching those goals. For instance, we said we wanted to be able to communicate better and to simply like each other better. In the enrichment workshop, the leader helped us plan how to reach those goals—including one evening a week eating out with each other and spending at least one hour just relaxing and talking. We also took some inventories which identified ways we could improve our communication skills.

Learning to set goals for our marriage has also helped us set goals with our kids. They really like knowing what's going on and enjoy working together.

More goodwill is generated in the marriage when husband and wife have similar goals or purposes, rather than diverse ones. Says one husband:

My wife's goal is to accumulate material possessions—a large, luxurious home, expensive cars, fancy clothes. I would really be more satisfied to live a simpler life and spend less time and effort on my job.

Tension is certain in marriages like this where spouses are constantly at odds about their goals and purpose in life and how their time, effort, and money are spent. On the other hand, when partners agree where they want to go in their marriage, they can figure out how to get there.

Expectations for the Marriage

Neither is variety the spice of life when marriage partners have different notions about what their marriage should be like and what each of them should be doing—or not doing—to create that marriage. For instance, a man who considers a "good" marriage one in which the husband's career is more important than the wife's, and all decisions are made on that assumption, is perfectly happy as long as his wife also considers this arrangement a "good" marriage.

But what happens when the wife's definition of a "good" marriage is different from that of her husband? Suppose she decides it is her turn to have a career outside the home. She has spent the first twenty or twenty-five years of their marriage rearing the children and helping her husband succeed in his career. Now she wants a chance to do something different. Unless the husband can understand and support her desires, and the two can work out a compromise, the marriage is in for some serious turbulence.

Similar obstacles to marital serenity may rear their ugly heads when the husband, or the wife, or both retire. Each frequently dreams of a quite different life after retirement than does the other. As one wife put it:

> I thought after Mel retired we could travel some, we could entertain friends, and we could do a lot of things together. Mel envisioned working in the yard and puttering around his shop while I prepare our meals, clean house, and run errands. His retirement was sure no "retirement" for me.

Mel's counterattack was one of surprise:

> I thought Elaine *wanted* to spend more time at home. In all those years she worked, she complained that she'd be glad when she had more time at home.

After Mel and Elaine leveled with each about their expectations for the retirement stage in their marriage, then they were able to work out a more congenial truce.

Variety in Ideas about Sex

Partners with very different notions about sex may spend their marriage career quibbling over two basic questions: "*How often* shall we have sex?" and "*What* shall we do?" Ron says, "I would really like to have sex more often than Sherry wants it." Sherry admits, "I don't want sex as often as Ron does, but when we do have sex, I need more time than Ron does for full enjoyment. . . ."

Another husband says, "Linda is so uptight about sex. She's afraid to try anything new or different. She forgets we're married. It's like her mother is in the picture frame over the head of our bed, and she's looking down on us with a disapproving scowl on her face as she shakes her finger at us and says, 'Nice girls don't. . . .' I just wish Linda could envision cross-stitched needlework in the frame reminding her of God's words: 'Therefore shall a man leave his father and his mother, and shall cleave unto his wife: and they shall be one flesh' [Gen. 2:24, KJV]."

Variety in Religious Beliefs

How important any religious belief or practice is for compatibility in the marriage is influenced by how important each partner *thinks* it is. For instance, if two people of different religions get married, they are bound to have collisions over their differences sooner or later if they both are strongly committed to their religious beliefs and practices. But if one or both of them is only nominally committed, then religion may not become a source of tension and conflict. On the other hand, if the partners are not active in their church and fail to practice their faith, they are robbing their marriage of a valuable source of strength. Consider this observation:

> Fifty percent of all couples wind up divorced. Of those who attend religious worship services together, only one in forty divorce. Of those who attend religious worship services and other activities such as Bible studies and prayer meetings, only one in 400 divorce.[1]

The Key to Peaceful Coexistence

My husband hates curried food. I love it. When I eat food seasoned with curry, that delectable blend of spices and herbs, thoughts of exotic, faraway places almost sweep me away. When Del eats curried foods, not only do his taste buds cringe in repulsion, but an insufferable case of indigestion almost kills him. He genuinely appreciates my not imposing my culinary preferences on him. I appreciate his treating me with the same consideration.

To coexist peacefully in marriage, it is best not to try to force your tastes, opinions, preferences, and ways of doing things on your mate. In some cases, unyielding insistence results in culinary discomfort. In other instances, the consequences are more serious, damaging, and lasting. Instead, respect your mate's right to feel, think, and act according to his or her own individuality. Then, rather than differences driving you apart, they can bring interest and vitality to your relationship.

Remember: When it comes to marriage, variety is not naturally the spice of life. You must season every platitude with a grain of salt. Even this one.

MYTH 7:

Marriage Is *Serious* Business

SEVERAL YEARS AGO *Newsweek* magazine recommended ten ways to cope with the pressures of the workplace. First on the list was "Maintain a sense of humor." I think this suggestion also deserves the rank of Number One in handling the pressures of marriage. Many marriage partners are burned out or washed out. They are pushed to the limit, stressed out, or teetering on the brink of the breaking point. Staggering under the heavy load of unyielding work schedules and oppressed by unrealistically romantic marital expectations, they live lives of quiet desperation.

Do not get me wrong. I believe couples do indeed need to take their vows to each other seriously; they should honor their commitment to God and to each other. But many would simply find life a lot more pleasant and agreeable and would be a lot happier if they had a better sense of humor.

Too many are so *dead serious* their marriages have no life, no sparkle, no laughter. They have forgotten how to relax, how to have fun, how to enjoy each other. Instead of taking themselves and each other so seriously, they need a lighter touch. They need to learn to loosen up and make

time in their hectic schedules and harried marriages to
laugh more. Solomon, considered the wisest of men ever
to live, emphasized:

> There is a right time for everything:
> A time to be born;
> A time to die; . . .
> A time to cry;
> A time to laugh (Eccles. 3:1–2, 4, TLB).

Humor is valued the world over; a familiar French adage
expresses it this way: "The most completely lost of all days
is that on which one has not laughed." Proverbs, those
"nuggets of truth" written to instruct the "already wise to
become the wiser" (Prov. 1:6, TLB), lend further support to a
lighter touch: "A glad heart makes a cheerful countenance"
(Prov. 15:13, RSV). And "a cheerful heart has a continual
feast" (Prov. 15:15, RSV).

What Is a "Sense of Humor"?

One dictionary defines a sense of humor as "the ability to
perceive, appreciate, or express what is funny, amusing, or
ludicrous." This definition indicates a sense of humor is
much more than superficial rip-roaring, backslapping trick-
ery or hilarity.

A genuine sense of humor is more like the deep joy the
apostle Paul meant when he listed it as the second fruit of
the spirit: "But when the Holy Spirit controls our lives he
will produce this kind of fruit in us: love, joy, peace, pa-
tience, kindness, goodness, faithfulness, gentleness and
self-control" (Gal. 5:22–23, TLB). Referred to countless times
in the Scriptures, joy is considered different from happiness. Bible scholars point out, "Happiness tends to come out
of circumstances that are happy while joy comes despite
circumstances, i.e., Paul and Silas were joyful in prison
(Acts 16:23–33)."[1]

Using joy as the closest synonym I can think of for sense
of humor, I think most happy marriages have a certain

degree of it. Phylliss McGinley agrees. In an article titled "Laughter in Our Family," she says, "Happy families are alike in many ways. For one thing, they own a surface similarity of good cheer. . . . And they usually have a purseful of domestic humor accumulated against rainy days. This humor is not necessarily witty. The jokes may be incomprehensible to outsiders, and the laughter springs from utterly trivial sources. But the jokes and the laughter are valuable because they belong to the families."[2]

In contrast, troubled families, families with no sense of humor, no joy, are described by Virginia Satir, noted family therapist: "In troubled families the bodies and faces tell of their plight. Bodies are either still and tight, or slouchy. Faces look sullen, or sad, or blank like masks. Eyes look down and past people. Ears obviously don't hear. . . . There is little evidence of friendship among [them], little joy in one another."[3]

A Sense of Humor Is No Laughing Matter!

The stark contrast of McGinley's happy family and Satir's troubled ones highlights the powerful influence of a genuine sense of humor in marriage. If a sense of humor is Number One—or even in the top ten requirements—for successful marriages, you would think the experts would have written a chapter or at least a paragraph or so in their books. Not so. I looked through twenty-seven marriage books, mostly college texts, before I concluded that these experts aren't serious about a sense of humor.

In my search, however, I did run across topics which piqued my curiosity as to how I could possibly have lived happily in a marriage for a quarter of a century with no knowledge whatsoever of these timely topics. Nearly every book index, for example, listed such terms as *Cowper's glands, mating gradient, propinquity, homogamy, structured functionalism, symbolic interactionism,* and theories of "escalators and dyadic crystallization."

My husband and I had a jolly good time speculating what these words might mean. We both concluded that it is no wonder the marriages of so many young people are coming apart at the seams if a knowledge of these terms is the glue that is supposed to hold them together. What well-intentioned marriage partners need to know is not so much about esoteric terms and theories, but hard core survival techniques, like how to instill a face-saving sense of humor into their relationship.

What Does a Sense of Humor Do?

A sense of humor helps put things into perspective. It keeps us from making mountains out of molehills. A sense of humor also allows partners the right to be less than perfect. An honest "Boy, I goofed" or a candid "I really blew it" helps your mate know that you are not perfect and, even more important, that you are willing to admit it. Just as important, you extend that same basic human right to your mate. The ability to laugh at yourself takes a lot of pressure off a marriage relationship.

A sense of humor is also a social lubricant. Recall the familiar saying, "Laugh and the world laughs with you"? Another saying I once heard put it this way: "Shared laughter creates a bond of friendship." Yet another expressed it this way: "Laughter is the shortest distance between two people."

All too often marriage seems to mysteriously rob partners of the spirit of fun and playfulness that marks their interaction with others, as well as the joy that marked their courtship. Perhaps it is the mistaken notion that marriage is such serious business that there is no room for good-natured fun and joy. Quite the contrary! Catherine and Loren Broadus, co-authors of PLAY—It's Not Just for Kids, state simply, "Laughing is a gift of God to help us live more joyously." They contend that a spirit of playfulness and comedy teaches us to look at life exactly as it is, undulled by scientific theories. Comedy banishes monstrous monotony from marriage while teaching us to be responsible, to be honest, to interrogate ourselves, and to correct our pretentiousness.

A spirit of fun also relieves stress, and consequently improves health. Undue tension can drive up blood pressure or exacerbate ulcers, back problems, alcohol and drug abuse, and anxiety. Choosing to live life with a sense of balance, good humor, and happiness, on the other hand, may be the most important health factor in life. Scriptures remind us of an age-old truth, "A cheerful heart does good like medicine, but a broken spirit makes one sick" (Prov. 17:22, TLB).

Seeing the Brighter Side of Things

Like many virtues, the ability to see the bright side of things does not always come naturally. If that is the case, the following tips may very well help you inject some levity into your marriage.

1. *Learn to lighten up, live a little, and laugh a lot.*
As a child, I thought many Christians were the saddest people around. It seemed to me that their philosophy of life was this: "If anything is fun—or funny—it must be sinful." Unfortunately, I still see some Christian couples consciously or subconciously living by this creed. In contrast, two of our best friends always seem so full of life, able to enjoy each other as a married couple, and to overcome the numerous crises that arise in their large family. I once asked Bob to what he attributed their happier-than-normal family life. Without hesitation, he responded, "We've learned to laugh a lot!"
Simply becoming aware of the nature of your attitude and making a commitment to lighten up, love a little, and laugh a lot is a gargantuan leap in the right direction. And remember, it takes fewer muscles to smile than to frown.

2. *Be sensitive to differences in sense of humor.*
Just as no two fingerprints or snowflakes are identical, so are we different in our interests, temperaments, and what tickles our funny bone. Del and I not only enjoy different cartoons and comic strips, we laugh at different

circumstances and incidents. At first Del considered me as having "a weird sense of humor," and I accused him of being "stodgy." Not only do I laugh easily, I also cry easily. The whole gamut of my emotions always lurks right beneath the surface, ready to explode on a second's notice. In contrast, Del's emotions are controllable, appropriate, predictable—"As emotions should be," he self-assuredly adds.

I have learned to draw strength from his stoic reliability. He has learned simply to tolerate my unpremeditated outbursts of hysteria. He knows I try to contain myself, but if I slip and laugh inappropriately, I have learned to say something to add dignity to the laughter. For example, the time Del fell out of the shower and again the day he backed our '65 Ford Mustang (our only "classic" possession) into a brick wall I managed to gasp, "I'm laughing because I'm so glad you aren't hurt!" What can he say to that? At other times when my weird sense of humor produces unseemly peels of laughter, I justify it by telling Del, "But you so seldom make a goon out of yourself, I have to laugh on those rare occasions."

If you and your spouse vary greatly when it comes to a sense of humor, just remember, for the sake of marital harmony, to be sensitive to those differences.

3. Consider Timing.

As in all great endeavors, timing is critical in the appropriate and productive use of your sense of humor. Never laugh *at* your mate; always laugh *with* him or her. As suggested earlier, if you absolutely cannot help but laugh when your mate is not laughing and does not appear to be close to doing so, try to say something loving to let him or her know your laughter is not meant to be unkind. Del reminds me occasionally of the importance of being in agreement about whether to laugh together—or not to laugh. To emphasize this he cut out a little saying and put it on the refrigerator under the frog magnet: "Together we stick; divided we're stuck."

Establishing Your Own Ground Rules

Aside from this never-to-be-broken rule of never laughing *at* your mate, the rules related to timing depend somewhat on the situation and what ground rules you and your marriage partner work out. Here are some of the ground rules Del and I have established for when to laugh, and examples of how these rules have salvaged the serenity of our marriage:

1. *When there is nothing you can do but laugh.*
One beautiful spring day Del and I were driving back to our home in Waco after visiting with his mother. One of the highlights of this monthly trip had always been to get a barbecued sandwich in a town halfway home. On this particular day we decided to "go all out." We bought barbecued chicken, baked beans, slaw, and cherry cobbler. We then drove out of town to a scenic roadside park. With tastebuds eagerly anticipating their treat, we spread our feast out before us on the table. "This park table has never seen such a spread," Del commented as I reached into the paper bag to get the handy plastic knives, forks, and spoons—or so I thought. "No forks?" I half asked, half stated, as I stared into the bottom of the empty bag. Have you ever been eight miles from nowhere with a banquet feast and nothing to eat it with? Any situation like this challenges your ability to improvise as well as your ability to perceive, appreciate, or express what is funny, amusing, or ludicrous. By the way, nothing strengthens the bonds of matrimony quite like the shared laughter of eating barbecued chicken and all the saucy trimmings with your fingers!

2. *When one or both of us do not understand what to do next.*
As academic nomads, and as two smitten with congenital wanderlust, Del and I have spent a great deal of our married life in a car. Del traditionally assumes the role of navigator. He likes to figure things out, and he is good at it. So I have relinquished all my map-reading rights to him. On

one of our trips, Del decided to temporarily abrogate the
wheel and take a nap. He had written out the highway
numbers to follow, and his last words before falling asleep
were, "You can't miss it." (I have since learned that anytime
this statement is made, I am *certain* to miss it!)

Quite unsuspecting, I drove into a metropolitan five-
o'clock rush hour and somehow ended up on one of those
archaic traffic circles. The traffic was four lanes deep with
cars entering the circle at high speed and leaving at even
higher speeds as they crossed at least two lanes but usually
four to do so. I could not take my eyes off the hundreds of
cars zooming around me to read the signs above me and
beside me. I shrieked, "What do I do?" Rising from a deep
sleep, Del peered out the window and said as he pointed,
"Follow that vehicle!" I laughed. I laughed hysterically.
There simply was nothing else to do. I certainly couldn't
follow the vehicle. It quickly disappeared in the rush. So we
went around a few more times. Then, given a few minutes
to get awake and get our bearings, Del directed us smoothly
off that awful muddled mixmaster.

That traffic circle incident gave rise to a slogan that we
use when choices are bombarding us from every direction
and we do not know what to do. First we laugh, and then
we chime in together, "Follow that vehicle!"

3. *When one of us has an overriding urge to kill the other.*
One old story survives simply because married couples
identify with it. Someone asked a couple on their twenty-
fifth or fiftieth wedding anniversary if either had ever
considered getting a divorce. One of the partners responded as the other's head nodded in complete agreement, "Divorce . . . no. Murder, yes!" Situations evoking
that response in my own marriage bring to mind several
incidents. Here are a few I incited:

• When I inadvertently put a golden furniture-polish-
  soaked rag into the washing machine with Del's wash-day
  white underwear.

- When I used Del's new toothbrush for a week because I thought he said he had bought it for me. (Why is it that sharing a toothbrush in the early honeymoon stage of marriage is romantic but grounds for the death sentence later?)

- When I sprayed Del's face (and his spotless new trifocals) on three consecutive days with the new kitchen sink attachment. (I warned Del before we got married that I wasn't particularly adept with mechanical devices!)

Here is the most recent "urge-to-kill" incident Del caused:

- When he left the shampoo for our beloved Lhasa Apso dog, Mandy, in an unlabeled plastic container in my shower. I discovered I'd been using dog shampoo only when I inquired of Del what kind it was so I could get more of it for my by-then more manageable hair.

Marriage partners usually do not laugh during emotion-laden moments (or hours, or days). But as a safety valve, it helps to laugh later, and to use these times as learning experiences, as reminders that even very good marriages suffer through such times but are stronger because they do suffer *through* them and *survive*. For instance, Del and I are able to laugh now and wonder how a million-dollar marriage was almost declared bankrupt because of the crushing urge to kill over a drawer full of golden underwear; one soggy, double-duty toothbrush; a water-spotted face and trifocals; and a small, break-proof bottle of dog shampoo that, after all, did include a rather nice white vinegar rinse.

4. *When you need to pre-set your mind to handle in a positive way a potentially negative situation.*
Case in point: For two years I worked with an alcoholic administrator. I never knew what to expect from her; her attitude, behavior, and decisions were irrational and erratic. On days I anticipated exceptional stress, Del would say to

me as I left for work, "Remember, you are the sober one!"
That little humor encouraged me to face whatever might
unfold that day.

   5. *When you need a safety valve to help heal the hurts of
   grief.*
   Sadness and tearfulness are associated with grief; but joy
and laughter play a life-affirming role, too. In my book
Because You Care, I wrote, "During the tense times of weep-
ing and mourning over the death of a loved one, laughter
can serve as a tension breaker and a safety valve. Sensitivity, of course, is required for the right place and timing for
humor. However, recollecting some of the amusing incidents shared with the deceased may be the golden touch
which lightens the heavy burden of grief."[4]
   Another example of the power of a sense of humor to
help heal is also found in *Because You Care*:

   Jonathan's parents found reminiscing difficult, but both
   said when they finally came to the point where they could
   talk about Jonathan's short life with others and relate what
   they had enjoyed about it, they felt they had reached a
   milestone in their grief recovery. And when they could
   chuckle with their other children and friends about some of
   Jonathan's boyish antics, they knew they had passed yet
   another constructive turning point in their healing.[5]

The Source of Genuine Joy

   Today, the focus on marriage is too often on the struggles. I do not intend to trivialize the strife and sadness
which plague many marriages. And I do not mean to minimize the seriousness of the nature of marriage. But I do
think it is a misleading myth to think marriage partners
need to take each other and themselves more seriously. I
simply contend that a sense of humor may indeed be as
helpful to marriage as *Newsweek* says it is to people trying
to cope with the pressures of the workplace.
   Christ himself used humor to open people's eyes to truth.
In *The Humor of Christ*, Elton Trueblood shows how Christ

used satire, irony, and paradox to help clarify profound ideas. Consider the humor in these thought-provoking passages:

Matthew 23:24—Straining a gnat and swallowing a camel
Matthew 19:24, Mark 10:25, and Luke 18:25—Camel through a needle's eye
Luke 6:39—The blind leading the blind
Matthew 8:22—Dead undertakers
Matthew 7:16 and Luke 6:44—Figs from thistles
Matthew 7:34 and Luke 6:41—Speck and log in the eye[6]

Christ's use of humor was always used to clarify and to increase understanding, never to hurt—thus it's an unsurpassed model for marriage partners. The teachings of Christ challenge us to concentrate on joys which do not pass away rather than on the inevitable griefs that are spurious and superficial. A foolproof mandate for marriage might be paraphrased from Nehemiah 8:10: "The Joy of the Lord is my strength."

Everyone needs the elixir of humor to survive. Marriage should not put us in a straitjacket designed to keep us from enjoying life and each other. An old Norwegian proverb remarked on the power of laughter to the individual. You might just try it and see if it is not equally helpful in marriage:

He who laughs, lasts.

MYTH 8:

Families Are Falling Apart
Because Women Are Working
Outside the Home

"MY HUSBAND WON'T let me get a job."

I couldn't tell whether the newcomer's comment was a lament, a pious proclamation, or a putdown. Twenty or so people crowded the patio in groups of four or five to enjoy the pleasant back-to-school autumn weather. Not everyone knew each other, so people were making the usual informal self-introductions. In my group the inevitable question was asked of the newcomer, "What do you do?"

"I am a full-time homemaker," she said. "I feel that women working outside the home is the reason families are falling apart."

My personal experience did not support her statement. Widowed in her early twenties, my grandmother had to work outside the home to keep her three young daughters together as a family. Widowed at age twenty-four, my mother had to work outside the home to support my brothers and me. Out of my circle of friends that autumn day, three had divorced, and none of these women had worked outside the home. Two of my happiest friends have jobs; three of my unhappiest, most depression-prone friends do not work outside the home. Concluding my hasty mental "research," I blurted out, "I work outside the home, and my family is not falling apart!"

A Growing Trend—Not a Passing Fad

A quick survey of the patio gathering showed that I was the oldest living female survivor of a two-career marriage. Del and I have been married almost twenty-five years, and I have worked outside the home all but two of those years— when Christi was an infant. Until Christi was in school full days I taught part-time—but I did work, and overall it was a positive experience in our family, not negative.

Perhaps that's why I felt the pressure that day on the patio to personally defend all the other working women. My audience was captive as I shared what I knew about this important topic. According to Arthur Norton, family demographer for the U.S. Census Bureau in Washington, D.C., 65 percent of all the women in America are in the work force, and the majority of all working women are in a two-career marriage. Nearly 15 percent of all families depend upon the woman as the only breadwinner. For these women, there simply is no choice but to work. I think all working women deserve a hearing.

More and more women are working outside the home. In fact, Eli Ginzberg, Columbia University professor and noted human resource specialist, says, "The single most outstanding phenomenon of our century is the huge number of women who are entering the labor force."[1]

At the same time, divorce has increased to the point where one out of every two marriages breaks up. Just because these two trends are occurring simultaneously does not prove that one is causing the other. To say that families are falling apart because women are working outside the home oversimplifies a complex situation, I told the other guests. For emphasis, I raised my voice and said, "We could as easily conclude that the real reason families are falling apart is because the father is always working and rarely spends time with the children."

Clearly, the issue of two-career families and family breakdown can get pretty complicated. And I could clearly see that my patio audience did not want any more figures or statistics. "One thing is for certain," I added, "this issue is sure wrought with a lot of emotion and definite opinions." Everyone agreed with that.

Possible Causes of Family Breakdown

"If working wives and mothers aren't the cause of divorce and family breakdown," someone probed, "what *is* the cause?" Everybody offered different opinions:

> "Mobility . . . everybody moves around so there's less family support and togetherness than there used to be."
> "Less stigma associated with getting divorced."
> "People feel they deserve to be happy; there's less pressure to stay married if they're unhappy."
> "Higher expectations for marriage fulfillment."
> "Looser sexual standards and behaviors."
> "Materialism . . . people put more value on *things* than on people and relationships."
> "Financial pressures. . . ."
> "Overemphasis on individualism, self-fulfillment, and looking out for Number One rather than on sharing and encouraging one another."
> "People don't know how to build a good marriage . . . they are told it takes work, but there are few courses to teach us. There are no requirements to prove competency to get a marriage license."
> "We live in a throwaway society today. If something doesn't work or we get tired of it, we throw it away— including marriages."
> "Weakening spiritual values . . . less commitment to marriage."

A Difference of Scriptural Interpretation

The last cause of family breakdown mentioned rekindled the newcomer's interest. She interjected, "There are Bible verses that say women belong at home." Her comment sent me back to the privacy of my own thoughts as I remembered a similar conversation recounted in a book called *Help Me God, I'm a Working Mother!*[2] A full-time homemaker had made a comment almost identical to that of the newcomer. In the book, the author, also a working wife, replies, "I leaf through my Bible, looking for exceptions. There was Mary, who chose the better part over Martha, who was cumbered about with much serving. There was Deborah, a political leader, and Anna, the prophetess."

My mind skipped to Lydia, a woman from Thyatira who worked at Philippi selling the famous purple dye from her native area that was so much in demand in the ancient world. Won to Christianity by Paul, Lydia and her friends formed the nucleus of the congregation at Philippi. She was not criticized for being a working wife. Quite the opposite!

Next, I thought of some verses from Proverbs 31 celebrating the working wife and mother. In The Living Bible translation, these verses from 10 to 29 came to mind:

> If you can find a truly good wife, she is worth more than precious gems! Her husband can trust her, and she will richly satisfy his needs. She will not hinder him, but help him all her life. She finds wool and flax and busily spins it. . . . She gets up before dawn to prepare breakfast for her household, and plans the day's work. . . . She goes out to inspect a field, and buys it; with own hands she plants a vineyard. She is energetic, a hard worker, and watches for bargains. . . .
>
> She sews for the poor, and generously helps those in need. . . .
>
> She is a woman of strength and dignity. . . . When she speaks, her words are wise, and kindness is the rule for everything she says. She watches carefully all that goes on throughout her household, and is never lazy. Her children

stand and bless her; so does her husband. He praises her
with these words: "There are many fine women in the
world, but you are the best of them all!"

As I finished my silent review of this favorite scripture
and savored the satisfaction it gave me that the Bible indicates it is okay to be a working wife, a soft-spoken husband
offered this comment: "The more we talk, the more I think
whether or not a wife works outside the home is a decision
she and her husband must make with divine guidance in
what's right for them." I thought what he said made good
sense. After all, only 5 percent of the married couples in the
United States fit the traditional family mold of husband as
breadwinner and wife as full-time homemaker with children at home. Circumstances differ from couple to couple,
so it seems reasonable that each couple should decide what
is best for them.

Common Problems

If a couple decides the wife will work outside the home,
common problems usually crop up. Extra demands on time
and energy seem to plague every two-career marriage. The
wife may try to do all the housework as well as a daily eight
hours on the job. The husband traditionally views housework as female work and may have trouble helping with it.
Maybe his wife does not want him to help her. She may
doubt her own value if he can do "her" work. Some husbands
say they cannot please their wife when they try to help with
the housework. A wife interrupted, "Our biggest problem is
that neither one of us wants to do the housework!"

Another threat to two-career marriages is what to do with
the kids during working hours. "Finding a reliable person to
baby-sit is the first challenge," pointed out the mother of
two. "Willingness to pay through the nose is the next one,"
added the mother of three. If the kids are in school while the
mother and father work, child care may not be a problem.
Instead, adequate supervision after school and until a parent gets home may be the challenge. "Handled right," noted

one person, "this time can help the children develop responsibility and independence."

Problems may come when children do not follow the usual schedule. "For example, when they are sick," said a working mother with three children, "who stays home? Who takes the child to the doctor? To the dentist?"

Another parent posed questions about other occasions when children need one or more parents during working hours: "Who leaves work to go to the parent-teacher conference? To the Christmas play? To weekly music lessons?" In a traditional marriage, the decision is easy: The mother's job always gives in to the demands of the kids. But women increasingly express commitment to their jobs, and husbands increasingly are compelled to help with the kids— sick or well. To survive a two-career marriage the husband and wife must make decisions that will be satisfying to both. Deciding who is going to decide and how the decisions are made is often more critical than the decisions themselves. One wife emphasized, "I just like to know that I am respected as a person and that my husband doesn't just assume he can make decisions which affect me without even consulting me!"

Some male egos may be too fragile to survive a two-career marriage. "What if my wife was more successful than I am?" said one candid husband. "Or what if she made more money than I did? That would take some real adjusting."

Some women may have difficulty adjusting, too, for they may be uncomfortable outside a traditional homemaker role. Society still judges a man by his job and a woman by her skills as a homemaker, companion, mother, and hostess. Some women may be frustrated if they do better in their jobs than their husbands.

By this point in our patio discussion any indifference or amusement had turned to earnest concern. One husband, perched precariously on the edge of his lightweight lawn chair, stared intently at a dandelion struggling to grow between the bricks of the patio. He was a casualty of a failed two-career marriage; but he was giving his best effort to a second one. He leveled with us: "You gotta have lots of heart-to-heart talks about what you want out of marriage and what you are willing to do to accomplish what you want."

Frances, a stolid Camp Fire leader and Cub Scout den mother, was the veteran of three jobs and one marriage— all of them good. "You'd better find a job you really like," she said. "Then you'll be more motivated to work out all the little problems that two-career families have. If you don't like your job, you become frustrated, maybe even bitter. Then you're no better off than the mother who stays at home with her kids and resents it."

This discussion reminded me of another excellent book I had recently read. In *Free to Stay at Home: A Woman's Alternative*, Marilee Horton makes this insightful observation:

> I am aware some women, like some men, thrive on high pressure—that's what makes them tick—but I also think those women often try to speak for all women. Others feel pushed into the marketplace and haven't the emotional or physical stamina to handle it all.

The crowd had almost forgotten that I was the expert on this topic. To remind them, I stated with a tone of authority: "If you do want to work outside the home, select a job or career with flexible or part-time hours. That may give a wife the best of both worlds. Being good in whatever you do gives you bargaining power. Encourage your daughters to get a good education and to prepare for a career that allows them to work part-time if they plan to combine marriage, children, and a career. Teach your sons how to help around the house and to shop and to cook. Your daughter-in-law will be eternally grateful to you!"

Few Good Role Models

As others contributed advice based on their own experiences, a big problem in surviving a two-career marriage became apparent: models of successful two-career marriages are not plentiful. And sometimes we think of a couple as role models, only to find out they're mere mortals just like we are!

Diane Mullens, mother of one and one on the way, looked at me and said, "When I see you at a party like this, or at church, or eating out—or any place—I always think to myself, *She really has her life put together! Why, she is the kind who probably has her Christmas shopping done by Thanksgiving . . . her husband trained to do the grocery shopping and to fold the laundry . . . her teenager taught to remove dishes from the bedroom before stuff starts to grow in them . . . her dog trained to make his own grooming appointment. She probably has her beds made before she leaves the house each morning, no dirty dishes in her sink, no skipped dental appointments, no dust balls lurking under her furniture, no frozen chicken bones stored in the freezer till garbage day. . . .*"

"Stop!" I laughingly commanded my friend. "You have me all wrong. Those are the very thoughts I have about you!" The ensuing patio conversation convinced me that flashes of a superwoman haunt most working wives. We see this paragon of perfection as someone who knits marriage, career, and motherhood into a satisfying life without dropping a stitch. Such an image overwhelms and tortures many of us with feelings of contemptible failure, regardless of how well we juggle the many facets of our own lives.

Marriage is a challenge at any speed, but having unrealistic and unreasonable expectations may be the speed that kills. Our patio discussion emphasized how partners— especially wives and mothers—must eliminate from their vocabulary these unrealistic attitudes or any similar ones:

"If I don't do it, it won't get done."

"If you want something done right, you have to do it yourself."

"I'd rather do something myself than have to ask you to do it."

These martyr-like attitudes are hard to change, but they are destructive at home and at work. They are the reasons that many working wives and mothers are physically exhausted and emotionally stressed out. They also are the reasons why many employees do not delegate responsibilities—even simple ones—to others.

A husband in the patio crowd commanded our attention: "Listen, this all reminds me that getting everything put up, put away, or cleaned up is not as important in the long run as how we feel about each other—and ourselves."

Surviving a Two-Career Marriage

Just as the conversation was getting profound, I had to excuse myself to go home. I had come to the party by myself. Del was out of town and would be calling home any time. Our teenage daughter would be getting home from a ballgame pretty soon, and I anticipated a demanding day at my office and needed a good night's rest.

My parting words packed more axiomatic meaning than even I realized at the moment I said them:

Surviving a two-career marriage sometimes means leaving the party before you want to.

MYTH 9:

Good Sex Makes a Good Marriage

"IT AIN'T NECESSARILY SO." These words from an old song say it well. Many people expect a good sexual relationship to be the foundation of a good marriage, but "it ain't necessarily so." Instead, just the opposite is truer: A good marriage relationship is the foundation of a good sexual relationship.

It's true that sex may be the initial attraction between two people. But over the years, couples who fail to develop some strong nonsexual bonds are usually the ones who find, to their dismay, that sex is not as satisfying as it once was. On the other hand, most couples who develop a fulfilling relationship in nonsexual areas seem also to enjoy a satisfying sexual relationship.

Some experts feel so strongly that a good relationship is of primary importance and good sex is secondary that they carry the idea a little further. They maintain that a good marriage relationship enables couples to tolerate less than satisfying sex. But good sex usually cannot compensate for a poor relationship. Couples with a good sex life but miserable in most other ways generally split sooner or later, or exist in a tumultuous love-hate relationship.

Keep Meals —and Marriage —Well Balanced!

My grandmother was known far and wide for her good cooking and for her exuberant *joie de vivre.* In her ninety-plus years, she outlived three husbands, all of whom adored her—as did everybody else. When asked once about her secrets of success, she responded, "Keep meals and your marriage well balanced!" Little did Grandmother know that she had summarized what social scientists have been saying a long time. That is, a life that is well balanced in all areas— from the kitchen to the bedroom—is generally the happiest one.

Social scientists often divide life into these different areas that influence a well-balanced life:

• Social

• Emotional

• Physical

• Intellectual

• Spiritual

Let's look at how nonsexual behavior in these areas affects the sexual relationship.

Social: How Mates Interact with Each Other

Social, according to the dictionary, describes all the various ways marriage partners interact with each other. Social elements exerting the most influence on sexual interaction include meeting each other's needs, communicating, setting priorities, settling power struggles, and handling social pressures.

Meeting each other's needs. Some behavioral experts say the most basic need of human beings is to *understand* and *to be understood.* Others use the words "love," "acceptance," "appreciation," "recognition," and "belonging." Different terms may be used to describe this deepseated longing all people have to be treated with dignity and respect. Whatever labels are used, marriage provides the social setting in which this need can be met. How well a partner meets the mate's need in nonsexual interactions has an incredible effect on their sexual interaction. Marge, a full-time homemaker, comments:

Ted always treats me like a special person, and we've been married twenty-one years. I don't mean he carries on or makes a big to-do about everything. But he tries to understand my point of view and respects my feelings. I want to be a full-time homemaker, for example, and he supports me—and sometimes defends me in front of my friends who are always pushing me to "get a job."

With three kids at home, Ted and I don't have much time together. But ever so often, he asks me for a date—he calls and gets a sitter, and we go out to eat and spend a few hours just talking. Of course, I could get a sitter and make all the plans, but the fact that he takes the initiative makes me feel really loved . . . that he really values me as a person and wants to be with me.

Our sex life has always been good, and I am convinced it's because Ted always tries to be understanding and nice to me, even when he is not interested in sex. We have some friends who always belittle each other, and they wonder why their sex life is disappointing. I think I'd resent it and really feel "used" if the only time Ted was nice to me was when he wanted sex.

Several scriptures describe how to meet the basic human need for love and understanding. "Kindness makes a man attractive" (Prov. 19:22, TLB) offers meaningful advice for all aspects of marriage but especially to the man who wants to be sexually appealing to his wife. Another scripture emphasizes how actions must enforce the "I-love-you" attitude: ". . . Let us not love with word or with tongue, but in deed and truth" (1 John 3:18, NASB). Another reminder that actions as well as words must be based sincerely on love is

found in the time-tested observation of the apostle Paul:
"If I speak with the tongues of men and of angels, but do not
have love, I have become a noisy gong or a clanging cymbal"
(1 Cor. 13:1, NASB).

Communication: reaching out. When marriage partners
are able to reach out to each other and to express themselves effectively in less emotion-laden nonsexual areas of
the marriage, these capabilities flow into the more subtle,
emotionally explosive area of sexual communication. When
mates have trouble communicating in the nonsexual arena,
then they are almost certain to suffer difficulties in the
sexual arena. Consider what Rick says about this:

> Jeanne and I have had a problem communicating from the
> very beginning. She always assumes I mean one thing
> when I mean something altogether different. She expects
> me to read her mind. I try to; but I have to guess what she
> wants because she won't ever tell me. When she does tell
> me something, her actions often send an opposite message.
> And she is always telling me what I am thinking—she's
> usually off base, but how can I convince her when she
> won't even listen?
>
> Like the other night—she said, "You don't love me as
> much as you used to, or you would want sex more often."
> Then she said she was tired and went to bed. I thought she
> really meant she was tired—that *is* what she said. But the
> next morning she was puffed up and would hardly talk at
> all. She said it was because I didn't follow her right to bed
> and try to make love to her.
>
> First of all, I was surprised that she said anything at all
> about sex because she usually refuses to talk about sex. She
> says talking about it takes the romance out of it. Our com-
> munication is lousy in general, and it really shows up when
> it comes to sex.

Setting priorities. People place sex somewhere in their
lists of priorities along with money, children, house, career,
and so on. Marriage partners experience sexual difficulty
when they place much more priority or much less priority
on sex than the mate does.

Nan, for instance, did not realize until she and her husband began talking about his dissatisfaction with their

infrequency of sex that she gained more satisfaction from "keeping house" than on developing a good sexual relationship. This attitude may have stemmed from childhood conditioning that "cleanliness is next to godliness." Since all Nan's friends and neighbors could *see* her clean house, and she felt it was a measure of her godliness, or success as a wife, she simply put a clean house higher than sex on her priorities.

Similarly, individuals may set their priorities by the philosophy that "work comes before play." People who spend long hours in demanding careers simply may not have sufficient time—or energy—to develop satisfying sexual relationships with their marital partners. If both partners are heavily involved in their careers, they may be satisfied to relegate sex to a low priority. Here is one person's viewpoint:

> When Robin and I both were extremely busy—she with the kids and I with getting started in my career—we didn't seem to notice the low priority relegated to sex. Then when she had more free time after the kids were in school, she made me feel that I was ignoring or neglecting her. But my career was still very demanding. Then when I felt some relief in my job, Robin was really involved in some community project. Sex for us really suffers when our priorities are miles apart!

Settling power struggles. When two partners engage in a tug of war over "who's boss," and struggle with each other over who "has the right" to make certain decisions, harmony and goodwill are jeopardized. Not only is the positive social climate dampened, but seething resentment often flows in strong and dangerous undercurrents throughout all aspects of the marriage.

These ominous underlying tensions may be most destructive in sexual interactions, because these aspects of marriage are especially sensitive to power struggles. One husband comments:

> When there is a spirit of give-and-take in the marriage generally, I think it is reflected in a comfortable give-and-take

attitude in the sexual interaction. But when partners haggle over who's the boss and who's the hired help, there are going to be bad feelings . . . and bad feelings about sex are worse than other bad feelings.

Another married person agreed:

I think power struggles kill the spontaneity and pleasure in marriage, and especially in sex. For example, when there's always a battle of the wills, both partners become defensive and demanding . . . and in sex when there's friction about who's going to be the passive one and who's going to be the initiator—if that cannot be passed back and forth— the fun is taken out of it.

Handling social pressures. Marriage is the social setting in which sex is sanctioned. No longer do partners ask, "Shall we, or shall we not?" In marriage the two basic questions on which partners must arrive at mutual agreement if their sex life is to flourish are, "How often?" and "What shall we do?"

Most mates bring to the marriage bed some pretty definite ideas about what the answers to these two questions "should" be. Society also exerts subtle "shoulds." If, for example, somewhere the partners read that the average couple has sex a certain number of times a month, they feel a gnawing tug to try for at least a time or two more. After all, who wants to be just "average" in a society that says to be "average" is actually to be mediocre? And who wants to be mediocre, especially when it comes to sex?

How couples grapple with the two basic sex questions of "How often?" and "What?" is a reflection of the larger context of their marriage relationship. When they try to meet each other's needs, strive for mutual understanding in their communication, try to set mutually agreeable priorities and work out their own mutually satisfying way of relating to each other, they will create a social climate in which their relationship flourishes. That social climate, in turn, nourishes mutually satisfying sexual interaction. Because a marriage is not a single, isolated entity or act but a weaving together of social strands.

Where Satisfying Sex Begins

What part of the body wields the most power in sexual experiences? *The head!* That's where satisfying sex begins—not in the glands or any other part of the body. The head determines all the emotions or feelings that color our sexual experience. Without the right thoughts, attitudes, and emotions all hopes for sexual satisfaction are in vain.

A critical corollary to this is that satisfaction with sex is colored by emotions expressed all over the house, not just in the bedroom.

Situational factors diminish sex for some who perhaps hold an unrealistic, immature, or romantic view of marriage. Just the practicalities of living together are enough to turn off sexual desire for some. Says one wife, "When I see Jay stuffing his mouth with popcorn, watching TV like a zombie, or leaving his clothes all over the house, desire for sex disappears."

In spite of a whole host of such factors that may diminish sexual desire, Dr. Harold I. Lief, director of the Marriage Council of Philadelphia, maintains that by far the leading reason sex turns cold in the marriage is the relationship itself. "Fifty percent of the cases I see are caused by marital interaction," says Leif. Whatever pleasure is experienced with sex is not sufficient to make up for the negative emotions associated with the total marital relationship. A bad relationship simply kills or badly maims desire.

Many couples let the demands of family, housework, career, and social activities drain all their time and energy, leaving little for sexual interaction. Sex squeezed in little snatches of time when energy is at a low point will be void of emotional richness; instead, it will be merely mechanical and predictably boring.

No marriage will be completely free of negative emotions from time to time, and accepting that fact is one element of a healthy emotional climate. And a healthy emotional climate is essential to longlasting and satisfying sexuality.

Cathedral Sex

Several years ago I wrote an article called "Cathedral Sex," which appeared in the *Journal of Religion and Health*.[1] I fully believed then what I wrote in that article, and I believe it even more now. Cathedral sex is how I described a high-level sexual relationship, one that is more likely when spouses have a marriage relationship built upon a broad base of God-like affectional interaction. This concept is represented by a simple line drawing:

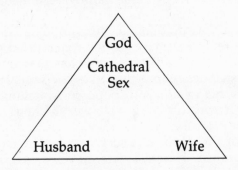

The closer the husband and wife are to God, the closer they become to each other, according to this concept. In practical terms, this simply means that the more the two mates put into their interaction with each other the qualities of God—love, caring, understanding, unselfishness, forgiveness, encouragement, and so on—the closer they grow toward each other and the stronger the bond of affection grows between them. When the total, overall relationship is filled with a lot of warm, caring interaction, it provides a broad-based, solid foundation for the sexual aspects of their relationship.

Because they have inherited misconceptions regarding wholesome sexuality, many Christian couples need to learn to *sanction* sex. That is, they need to learn to grant approval to themselves to have sex as husband and wife. Marriage partners need to learn to talk freely about what they enjoy.

They also need the emotional and psychological safety to talk about their sexual concerns and to discuss with each other any negative aspects of their sexual relationship.

Marriage partners may also need to learn that they have the right to *enjoy* their sexual relationships. This may often be seen as a wife's problem, but men may suffer from this misguided thinking, too. All too often it is men and women who have been reared in strict, so-called religious homes who seem to have the most difficulty granting themselves the right to enjoy sexual relationships with their spouse. Several husbands in a marriage enrichment workshop sponsored at our church said their wives fell into this category. One of the husbands said it was as though his wife could not accept the fact "that God knew what He was doing when He made our human bodies the way He did."

Some spiritual principles and specific scriptures which reinforce the fact that God did indeed know what He was doing when He designed the human body may be helpful. (See chart, p. 76.)

Most couples *intellectually* accept these scriptures and the spiritual principles long before they accept them *emotionally*. Reading and talking together about these principles helps many couples accept them emotionally. Some particularly good books are listed in an appendix at the end of this book.

When you are tempted to think that good sex makes a good marriage, remember, "It ain't necessarily so." Instead, working on the marital relationship itself holds the most reliable promise for good sex. When the marital relationship is strong, good sex is a natural expression of these positive feelings.

Celebration in the Bedroom, a beautiful book by Charlie and Martha Shedd, also contends that a good sex life is the result of a good relationship and, even more specifically, that a sound spiritual life enhances sex life. If you care about your marriage, consider putting into practice the Shedd's wisdom:

Spiritual Principles	Specific Scripture
1. God made man and woman for each other.	"And the Lord God said, It is not good that the man should be alone; I will make him a help meet for him" (Gen. 2:18, KJV).
2. God designed man and woman for sexual union.	". . . and they shall be one flesh" (Gen. 2:24, KJV).
3. God provides freedom to enjoy the body of your mate.	"And they were both naked, the man and his wife, and were not ashamed" (Gen. 2:25, KJV).
4. God sanctioned sex within marriage.	"Then God looked over all that he had made, and it was excellent in every way . . ." (Gen. 1:31, TLB). "Let marriage be held in honor among all and let the marriage bed be undefiled . . ." (Heb. 13:4, NASB).

Any couple not now praying together
Who will set aside a few moments each day
To sit quietly, discuss their feelings, then pray together
    silently;
Any couple who will do this for thirty days
Will experience improvement in every aspect of their
    relationship
And especially they will sense an exciting new dimension in
    their sex life.[2]

MYTH 10:

Couples Need to Plan More for the Future

"DON'T WISH YOUR life away!"

These words echoed in my ears and mind when I was a sixth-grade girl clinging to every word spoken by our teacher, Mr. Weir. Driven by bursts of energy like sparks from a frayed electrical cord, I always looked to the next activity, the next class, the next whatever. When I worked on arithmetic, I was already worrying about spelling. When I should have been concentrating on my studies, I was wondering, *Won't recess* ever *get here?*

Not only was I guilty of wishing class periods away, I was wishing away a year at a time! As a sixth grader, I longed to be a seventh grader. One day several of us were commiserating and predicting how much happier we surely would be next year. Overhearing our comments, Mr. Weir interjected those wise words, "Don't wish your life away! You're just like a bunch of butterflies fluttering from one blossom to another, never staying long enough to enjoy the beauty of the flower you happen to be on at the time. Learn to recognize what is the right thing to be doing each moment and give it your best effort and attention. Then the future will take care of itself."

It's Later Than You Think

"Don't wish your life away." As I have worked my way through nearly five decades of life and three university degrees dealing with human behavior, I have grown to appreciate even more the wisdom of Mr. Weir's words. Impetuous sixth graders, I have observed, are not the only ones who wish their lives away. Kathy, an older married student in one of my university classes, made this observation:

> I couldn't wait to get out of high school so I could go to work. Then I felt if I didn't get married, I would just die. Then I couldn't be happy until we had a baby right away. After three babies in five years, I could hardly wait till they all got in school so I could get back into the adult world of work. Then I grew impatient; I wanted them to get through school so I could quit work . . . looking back now I realize I spent some of the best years of my life wishing my life away.

Ben, a gentle but successful individual who worked in a fiercely competitive business, had given a lot of thought to his life. Consider what he had to say:

> I worked hard all my life; I never developed hobbies . . . didn't have time for them. "I'll do this . . . or that . . . when I retire," I told myself. I didn't spend much time with Evelyn . . . too busy working my way up in the business. Then Evelyn got sick with cancer . . . the slow, tortuous kind. One year after she died, I retired. I have regrets, mountains of them. I wish I had spent more time with my kids. They're grown now, and I hardly know them. I wish I had spent more time with Evelyn. I wish I had spent some time developing some interests, some hobbies. I had always thought I'd do these things later. Now it's "later," and it's too late.

The idea that couples need to plan more for the future is a particularly dangerous myth. Couples who do not plan at

all for the future, of course, are courting disaster—both financial and emotional. However, also teetering on the brink
of disaster are those couples who postpone building their
marital relationship, thinking they will spend more time
with each other "later." They fail to recognize the warning
expressed in the old saying, "It's later than you think." They
do not consciously decide to starve their marriage to death.
It simply happens over time as they push into the future all
the important plans they had for their marriage, all their
good intentions, all their hopes and dreams. And, like my
sixth-grade friends and me, they "wish their lives away,"
failing to enjoy their present relationship to its fullest.

A workaholic is a prime example of one who cannot relax
and enjoy the present unless he or she is working. Work-
aholism is a chronic disease which if untreated tends to be
terminal to marriages, because relationships get neglected
when one is smitten with this malady.

Let's Go Bug Hunting

Mr. Weir had urged his students to "recognize what is the
right thing to be doing each moment, and then give it your
best effort and attention." But one fall afternoon years later
I forgot Mr. Weir's words. I had rushed home from the
university where I taught and prepared a hasty dinner. I
threatened my daughter Christi to hurry and finish her
homework, "or else," and I reprimanded Del for leaving his
dusty shoes on the good carpet. I then frantically vacuumed
the entry way because a group of prestigious ladies were
coming by to pick up some good used clothing for a worthwhile cause. After that, a graduate student would be coming to our house to work on a very important thesis—one I
was certain would make a sound contribution to research.

As I paused to catch my breath, I heard Christi talking
with a friend on the telephone. Her comments went something like this:

Mom is cleaning house—some ladies we don't even know
are coming to pick up some old worn-out clothes. And a

college student is coming to work on a thesis . . . No, I
don't know what a thesis is, I just know Mom isn't doing
anything *important* . . . and she won't go bug hunting
with me.

Before Christi had hung up the phone, I had put on my
jeans and old tennis shoes, persuaded Del to do likewise,
stuck a note on the door telling the graduate student I
would be back soon, and set the box of used clothing on the
front porch with a note on it saying that Del, Christi, and I
had gone bug hunting.[1]

Even though Christi is grown now, when Del or I get
bogged down in our work and our marriage needs some
attention, one or the other of us recalls the magic of that
long-ago moment. That's when one of us offers the other a
simple invitation that carries mountains of meaning: "Let's
go bug hunting." Children have a way of making complicated and confused matters suddenly very clear.

There's a Right Time for Everything

Called the Father of Medicine, Hippocrates was a Greek
physician who lived several hundred years before Christ.
The Hippocratic Oath, the ethical code for the medical
profession, is attributed to him. Hippocrates is also given
credit for some words on the art of living. I think they
especially apply to the art of living in a marriage: "Life is
short, the art long, timing exact, experience treacherous,
judgment difficult."

This thought has been echoed throughout the centuries
by others. A book called *The Precious Present* by Spencer
Johnson says it this way: "It is also wise to think about the
future and to prepare for my future. But it is not wise for me
to *be* in the future for that . . . is how I lose myself." The
author emphasizes the importance of savoring each moment in your life and adds, "The present moment is the only
reality I ever experience." Scripture expresses this ageless
wisdom simply and clearly: "There is a right time for everything" (Eccles. 3:1, TLB).

We Won't Always Have Another Tomorrow

Sometimes it takes a tragedy—a death or divorce or some other heart-wrenching trial or tribulation—to make us realize how valuable the present is. Only then do we realize that we won't always have another tomorrow. My friend Frank Gentsch learned this important truth before he married, and it has served him well. But he learned it the hard way. Let me share his story:

Tubes jutted out of Frank. Needles jabbed in. Bright lights burned his eyes. Strange noises exploded like bombs in his ears. Formless people in white jackets hovered over him. The hospital room echoed endless, dizzying sounds and sights. *Is this what dying is like?* he asked himself as consciousness slipped away.

Not far away, Police Chief Larry Scott struggled to swallow as he looked straight into the strong, serious faces of his fellow police officers. Then he told them, "It's going to take *a dozen miracles* to pull Frank through."

Frank had always dreamed of being a policeman. Ever since he was a little boy, he had looked forward to the day when he would be called "Officer Gentsch." Graduation from the Waco, Texas Police Academy on October 1, 1981, was the fulfillment of that dream. On June 7, 1982, he had celebrated his twentieth birthday. "On top of the world" described the way Frank felt on June 19, 1982, as he made his rounds.

It was a sunburn, blistering hot day. When Frank saw a fellow shuffling along in a heavy rain coat, he immediately labeled him as suspicious. *Why would anyone,* Frank remembers thinking, *be wearing a bulky coat on a sweltering June day in Central Texas?*

Stepping out of his patrol car, Frank said, "Stop. I need to talk to you." The man walked on, a little faster, ignoring Frank's order. More emphatically, Frank commanded, "Stop right now, I need to talk to you!" When Frank saw him put his hand inside his coat, he asked, "What do you have there?"

"A gun," the man growled as he swirled, and pointed a large, shiny revolver straight at Frank and opened fire. The first bullet hit Frank's right arm. Frank knew this, not because of any pain, only because he could see the big hole the bullet had ripped in his arm. The next bullet drove into Frank's chest, right below his shirt pocket. Again, he felt no distress or discomfort.

Frank mused, *getting shot isn't so bad.* Then he saw the red blood oozing out of his chest onto his light blue shirt, and he remembered the two police officers who had been wounded in the last forty-eight months in this area. One of them had died. The question raced through Frank's mind, *Am I going to be statistic Number Two?*

The gunman ran into a deserted building. Other police officers responded quickly to Frank's call for help, several arriving on the scene almost immediately. After several short, horror-filled minutes, the ordeal was over.

Chief Scott pointed out later, "We found seventy-six live rounds of .22-caliber ammunition on the assailant, enough to kill all the officers who had come to Frank's aid and every spectator the shootout had attracted."

Wondrously, the gunman hit only two people—Frank and another officer who was shot in the leg. The other officer healed quickly and was soon back on the job; but Frank remained in the hospital for seventy days, playing a continuous game of tag with life and death.

Miraculously, Frank survived three major operations, and several close encounters with death. The doctors said his determination helped pull him through, but Frank was convinced that the concern, prayers, and other loving actions of so many people created in him the desire and will to live.

"I learned a lot about life from my brushes with death," Frank commented. "Ironically, my being shot made me even more positive than ever that I wanted to be a policeman. But those bullets pumped into me made me realize something even more important: I knew that I wanted to quit taking things—and people—for granted. I was resolved to enjoy

life more each and every day. When I married, this resolution was put to the test. I still wanted to be a good police
officer, but I also wanted to be a good husband. Both require a lot of time and attention—*right now,* not tomorrow,
not next month, not next year, but *right now.* Daily I am
reminded by the bullet fragments still somewhere in me not
to put important things off—we never know when we
won't have another tomorrow."[2]

Savor Each Moment

Shirley Temple Black based her life on the philosophy of
savoring the present. As a young movie star Shirley Temple
enjoyed immense popularity and could undoubtedly have
continued that success as an adult; but she withdrew from
the public, married Charles Black, and focused her life on
her family—which in time included three children.

People who knew her described Shirley Temple Black as
a well-balanced, content person. When someone asked her
about being so happy in the movie industry and then in
her marriage and family life, she shared a story about her
mother-in-law which perhaps reveals the secret of her own
contentment. When her husband Charles was a young boy,
he had asked his mother what was the happiest moment in
her life. She answered, "Right now."

Charles reportedly began quizzing his mother about
other moments that are traditionally happy. For example, he
asked, "What about the day you were married?" She replied,
"My happiest moment *then* was *then.* . . . You can only
live fully the moment you're in. So to me that's always the
happiest moment."

Married couples often wait till retirement to travel, to
read a certain book, to grow a garden—to devote themselves to enriching their marriage. But Arthur Norton, demographer with the National Census Bureau, notes that
many marriage partners fail to make it to retirement as a
couple. Even though the overall divorce rate has leveled off,
divorce among couples over age forty is still increasing.

And Norton adds, "Plans for retirement are also frequently disrupted by the death of one of the partners."

As I think about the different theories explaining how satisfying marriages develop, about Frank Gentsch's story, about Shirley Temple Black's experience, and about what Art Norton says, I think we may sometimes put too much stake in the future. To be sure, we do need plans for the future; but we might well profit by learning to savor each moment more fully. Or in the time-proven words of Mr. Weir:

> *Learn to recognize what is the right thing to be doing each moment and give it your best effort and attention. Then the future will take care of itself.*

MYTH 11:

Wedding Rituals
Are Just for Show

NOT LONG AGO, some friends invited me to attend their wedding—the second for both. Hence the ceremony had a poignant promise of the future in it, like a second chance at a new beginning. That marvelous old chapel—its rich mahogany benches and beams gleaming with a patina of the past and the multicolored stained-glass windows filling the air with rainbows—echoed romance and remembrance of other couples who there had celebrated the oldest of human ceremonies: the wedding. Long-ago voices seemed to speak softly of the continuing flow of generations as the man and woman repeated their vows.

"Tradition," the groom had said. *"We want tradition."* The bride had nodded her head in agreement. They unknowingly voiced the universal deep human need for affiliation and affirmation. In today's fast-paced world of unending change and fleeting, fickle relationships, people still seem to yearn for some constancy, solidarity, stability, and reliability. They yearn for tradition. Unfortunately, however, some couples who repeat the traditional marriage vows simply fail to give them serious consideration.

In his book *Family and Civilization,* Harvard sociologist
and historian Carle C. Zimmerman compared the disin-
tegration of various cultures with the parallel decline of
family life in those cultures. He identified eight specific patterns of the downward spiral, and one stood out as if it were
a flashing neon sign: Traditional meaning of the marriage
ceremony is lost.[1] My friend, the groom, spoke to this point:

> My first marriage got off to the wrong start. I had no sense
> of responsibility to my marriage partner or to the marriage.
> I had no sense of the solemnity of the vows we spoke. This
> second marriage is going to be different. I now realize the
> seriousness of the pledge and the commitment we're mak-
> ing to one another.

The Modern Need for Tradition

Marriage partners who honor the longstanding values of
love, trust, and commitment, beginning with the wedding,
and who continue to develop meaningful rituals throughout
the years of their marriage seem to enjoy a cohesiveness
and a sense of family that holds them together. In contrast,
couples whose attitudes and actions fail to reflect these
values seem almost doomed from the beginning. Today's
mobility, impersonal mechanization, and declining morals
make rituals and tradition even more meaningful and purposeful than in yesteryear. Consider what this friend and
marriage counselor as well as wife and mother has to say
about the matter:

> Family members need tradition and rituals more than ever
> to give them a sense of belonging and togetherness. A wed-
> ding, I think, is a dramatic expression of commitment to
> each other and is a public, purposeful way for couples to
> start out their lives together. But the wedding is just the
> beginning. Marriage partners need to continue developing
> rituals and traditions to strengthen their family ties. Rituals
> can be anything as simple as drinking coffee together be-
> fore leaving for work, laughing together at a family joke,
> playing games together, going on a picnic on the first day of

spring, or worshiping together, particularly on special holidays like Christmas or Mother's Day. I think rituals and
tradition serve an important purpose—beginning with the
wedding rituals!

A word of caution! Some people today tend to think
the more glorious and expensive the wedding pageantry,
the deeper the love and the more glorious the marriage. Not
so. When the marriage partners keep their commitment to
each other as expressed in their wedding vows, when they
nurture their love for one another, when they develop their
own traditions and a sense of family—*then* the more glorious and more lasting the marriage. All the symbolisms that
make up the wedding pageantry have no miraculous power
within themselves. They are simply tangible reminders of
all the love and commitment required to help marriage partners withstand the pressures, problems, and pitfalls wrecking so many marriages nowadays.

As my friends spoke of tradition, I wondered specifically
about the rituals of the wedding—*the music, the rings, the
attendants, the candles, the kisses, the cake.* Why is it that
these symbols and rituals have helped celebrate and seal
the marriage vows of couples throughout the ages? How
do they add meaning and solemnity to the wedding vows?
These questions sent me on a search that turned up some
interesting information on the origins of these traditions. It
seems that some of our modern wedding rituals reflect only
a glint of their original meaning, but they still meet an
important human need in symbolizing an outward expression of an inner commitment.

The Oldest Symbol

The wedding ring is probably the oldest and most universal marriage symbol. This practice evolved from ancient
people merely breaking a coin in half, and each partner
taking the matching half. The Romans and Greeks used
wedding rings, and rings have been found in ancient Egyp-
tian tombs.[2]

People generally wore the ring on the left hand. Since most individuals were right-handed, they considered the left hand inferior. Wearing the ring on the left hand was thought to denote submission and obedience. Which finger should display this symbol of highest friendship was unsettled. Some say the ring was worn on the first finger, then the middle, and only later on the ring finger as we know it. One reason for wearing the ring on this finger was the belief that it has a small artery in it which leads straight to the heart, making it the most proper finger to bear a pledge of love.

In some cultures the man wore the engagement ring, not the woman. Perhaps the man continued to wear the ring as long as it symbolized power and authority. But when it became a visible sign of bondage and took on the meaning of obedience, then the woman began wearing it. Doublering ceremonies reflect the current emphasis on the sharing and mutuality of modern marriages.

The "band of gold" has not always been gold. In ancient times it was iron. In the Middle Ages, poorer people used rings made of rushes or other plants having hollow stems. Only in the seventeenth century did social pressure dictate that the ring should be gold, pure and non-tarnishing.

Lovers have not always given rings with valuable stones. In earlier cultures, people feared that a monetary value would be placed on the ring. And this would be inconsistent—or even an insult—to the love they felt was immeasurable. The diamond first was worn as the birthstone for April. Since the diamond stood for innocence (especially for women) and was durable, it evolved into the fashionable wedding gem. The diamond also was thought to guard against temptation from Satan. Even so, the Puritans' feelings against wearing wedding rings were so strong that they tried to abolish them.[3]

But they failed. Today the ring is more widely used than ever. In fact, it is looked upon almost as a necessity in the marriage ceremony, though it is not required by law. The ring's circle shape symbolizes never-ending love, and most brides and grooms claim this promise by giving rings to each other as the words "With this ring I thee wed" are spoken.[4]

Witnesses

Witnesses and a public kiss have nearly always been part of the pledge to each other voiced in the wedding ceremony. These witnesses were probably forerunners of the male and female attendants we now see in most modern weddings. Today, the bride's attendants often help her get into her wedding attire, and after the wedding they may help her change to her going-away outfit. Before honeymoons became customary, in the seventeenth century, it was also the duty of the groom's attendants to undress the groom. One historian described the high point of these responsibilities: "And then both groups saw to the placing of the new couple side by side in bed."[5]

To the relief of most twentieth-century couples, the time and place of the sexual consummation of the relationship is no longer a public affair. One Victorian writer contended that people (particularly brides and grooms) never fully accepted this practice and that the original task of the groomsmen probably was to defend the bridegroom against a rival who might carry off the bride.[6]

Giving Away the Bride

As for the other participants in the wedding party, the father's "giving away" the bride is rooted in the notion that the father "owned" his daughter until he had chosen a worthy marriage partner to "give" her to. In olden times the dowry was a vital part of this custom. Today the only remnant of a dowry is the hope chest, which also is fading as couples depend more upon wedding gifts to partially furnish their first household.[7]

Children

Children in the wedding party were included to encourage fertility. They were a reminder of an age-old purpose of marriage. Most couples place no stock in this symbolism. They generally invite people, including children, to be in their wedding because they are special friends or relatives.

The couple wants these persons to share and celebrate their pledge of love and commitment to one another—nothing more, nothing less.

The Wedding Kiss

As for the wedding kiss, its original purpose was to seal or affirm the commitment. The kiss is not required today to make the marriage legal. In earlier times, the priest gave the groom the "benediction kiss," the "kiss of peace," or the "holy kiss," as some called it; the groom in turn then kissed the bride. The priest's assistants then solemnly kissed each of the wedding guests. Nowadays the wedding participants and guests seem to prefer doing their own kissing.

Candles

Candles or torches have enhanced weddings through the ages. By the time the spirited wedding procession in ancient Rome got under way, it was usually dark. Thus the torch-bearers who escorted the party served a double function. The torches lit the way through dark city streets and also symbolized the enduring flame of marriage. Later, in Christian marriages, the wedding was in the sight of God, whose presence was symbolized by a single blazing candle, substituted for the ancient wedding torch of the Greeks and Romans.

Candles may merely add beauty or romance to contemporary weddings. In other ceremonies, couples attach religious symbolism to the lighting of their individual candles from one large candle—or the reverse, with the two individuals holding single candles and lighting one larger candle. The rituals may symbolize two becoming one, or portray the source of their love for each other as God's unending supply of love.

The Bride's Veil

Christian, Jewish, Moslem, and Hindu brides have used veils in their weddings. Historically, the veil protected the

bride against malicious spirits and from the "evil eye."
It also symbolized her protected purity, a kind of gift wrap-
ping. Pulling the veil back after the vows denoted the
bride's new status as a wife.

Wedding Gown Color

The color of the wedding gown has been significant
through the ages. The white wedding dress has traditionally
symbolized the bride's virginity. A remnant of this guarantee is the practice of the bride's wearing another color for
any subsequent marriages.

Cutting the Cake

Can you imagine a bride wearing ears of corn as the
finishing touches for her lovely wedding ensemble? Centuries ago, ears of corn were worn to entice the gods who
were believed to control fertility. It seems like a long leap,
but actually wearing ears of corn was the forerunner of the
cutting of the wedding cake by the bride and groom, one of
our oldest and most widespread customs.

Ancient people believed that breaking or cutting the cake
magically facilitated breaking the bride's maidenhead and
aided the birth of the first child. Breaking the cake over the
bride's head was customary until a milder and less messy
practice of sprinkling some of the crumbs on her became
sufficient. Evidently this is also the source of the practice of
throwing rice, colored confetti, or birdseed on the couple.[8]

Flowers

Flowers always have been important in the wedding ritual. The bridal garland, originally olive or myrtle, is probably the oldest part of the wedding costume and was a
tribute to the bride's virtue. In the Middle Ages noble brides
wore their finest jewelry, but peasant brides wore their
favorite flowers. In ancient France the father of a girl with
no dowry would tell prospective grooms that "her fortune
would be her garland."

The Victorians took the garland from the bride's head and made it into a bouquet. Even earlier, industrious mothers had started using flowers in other ways. For instance, they decorated the bride's house as well as the groom's with olive and laurel leaves as symbols of abundance and virtue. This practice was perhaps a forerunner of decorating the altar in the church with flowers and greenery.

Wedding guests once scattered flowers from the house of the bride along the road to the church. A remnant of this practice is seen today in the flower girl who strows flower petals or colorful bits of paper resembling flower petals before the bride walks down the aisle.

Discouraging Evil Spirits

Having someone other than the bride walk down the aisle during the wedding rehearsal is based on early attempts by the bride to avoid evil spirits. The comment that "it is bad luck" to walk through one's own wedding rehearsal is enough to keep many brides from doing it. Leaving the wedding altar through the same door the bride entered also is founded on the belief that to do otherwise would be unlucky.

Another good-luck custom is placing a coin dated the year of the bride's birth in the bride's shoe. Traditionally this was to ensure wealth in the marriage. Most brides today put little faith in this custom, but continue it anyway. Another custom taken even less seriously is for the groom to carry the bride across the threshold. It has its origins in the days when daughters were owned by their fathers. Carrying the bride across the threshold symbolized transfer of ownership.

Other traditions have also lost sight of their original meanings. Milder than ever, for example, is today's charivari—the forcible separation of the bride and groom after the wedding ceremony, painting the car with shaving foam or shoe polish, putting rocks in the hub caps, or even disconnecting part of the engine so the couple cannot make a dramatic getaway, short-sheeting the bed or tying a cowbell under it, tying old cans or shoes to the rear of the car, or chasing the couple out of town after the wedding. These acts undoubtedly relate to the ancient and honorable custom of frightening the devil away from the newlywed couple. Perhaps charivari has died down because experience proved that the couple did not particularly appreciate the help.

Outward Expression of Inner Feelings

Wedding rituals today may not symbolize what they did in yesteryear nor serve the same purpose per se. Perhaps today they serve a more profound purpose: They are symbols of the couple's mutuality and commitment. Most importantly, they are an outward expression of that inner feeling called love. And today, more than any other time in human history, love is the impelling force behind marriage. Perhaps with more outward expressions of that love, beginning with the wedding rituals and extending through other rituals and tradition throughout the marriage, the relationship can be made more fulfilling and longer lasting.

The tone of the *marriage* is at least partly set by the *wedding*. As John Heywood, a fifteenth-century writer, said, and it may well be true:

Wedding is destiny.

MYTH 12:

Holidays Are Joyous Times That Bring Family Members Closer to Each Other

SEVERAL YEARS AGO during one particularly hectic holiday season, Del and I attended the deacons' annual Christmas banquet. Whether or not to go had been a tough decision. Our teenage daughter had a basketball game that same evening, and we always tried to see her play. However, she insisted that she wanted us to go to the banquet, saying that she probably wouldn't even get to play. We finally concluded that not going to the banquet just wouldn't look right—we wouldn't be upholding our image of "good" Christians.

As it turned out, our daughter made a critical point in the last seconds of the game. And we missed that memorable moment because we were listening to a speech on how we all should be spending more time with our children, especially during the Christmas holidays.

Holidays are joyous times that bring family members closer to each other. Myth or maxim? Unfortunately it's mostly myth.

Unrealistic Expectations

Great expectations are generally held for holidays and vacations, but in reality these high hopes frequently come crashing down on family members as they did on Del and me that evening of the Christmas banquet and our daughter's ball game. Already busy schedules are frequently stretched beyond their limits with frenzied activities and social obligations—like deacon's banquets—that pull family members in a million different directions. As a result, all too often holidays leave families physically exhausted and spiritually disillusioned rather than refreshed and rejuvenated and knitted closer together.

Take Christmas, for example, the holiday that epitomizes all others. As we enter the Christmas season, television shows portray happy families getting together. Advertisements feature poses of perpetually pleasant people. Christmas cards depict pastoral scenes, often with sparkling snowflakes floating peacefully down on cottages with ribbons of smoke unfurling from the chimney. And we assume, of course, that inside are loving family members, bodies warmed by the crackling logs, and hearts touched by all the cozy togetherness.

The *real* Christmas season, in contrast, is described quite differently by many people. The comment of one distraught individual sums it up well, "The Christmas bustle has turned into the Christmas hassle." In studies of loneliness by John Woodward at the University of Nebraska, Christmas, the season of love, is decried by many not as the *loveliest* but as the *loneliest* time of the year. Countless individuals admit to having one or more of these feelings:

1. "Everyone else" has someone who cares about them.
2. "Everyone else" is getting the gifts of their hearts' desire.
3. "Everyone else" is having a wonderful time throughout the holidays.

Some psychologists say the peak suicide season is April, after the seeds of despair and self-destruction have been

planted in the holiday seasons, including Christmas and
New Year's. During these festive times, expectations soar so
high that when impossible dreams are not fulfilled, despon-
dent individuals sink into even deeper intolerable lows.

Career and jobs keep some people from going back to
their hometowns for the holidays, and "they miss the feeling
of rootedness and home at the holiday times," says Herbert
Freudenberger, a New York psychoanalyst. He adds, "It's
the other side to success, and it hits hardest in the Christmas season."[1]

Those who do make it "home for the holidays" may face
other disappointments. Florence Kaslow, a psychologist in
West Palm Beach and director of the Florida Couples and
Family Institute, says, "Some people go home to their parents wanting things unchanged from the past, and others
go home wanting everything totally different."[2] When their
expectations are out of line with reality, they set themselves
up for disappointment. Here is what one marriage partner
had to say:

> Every year I look forward to holidays and to vacations—and
> every year I am disappointed afterward. I think I simply
> expect too much, or I expect too much of the wrong thing.
> For example, we always try to see our parents during the
> Christmas holidays; we think it's important for our children
> to be with their grandparents and to get to know them bet-
> ter. But things never work out as great as we had them built
> up in our minds. Frankly, we are all at each other's throats
> before it's all over, and we're all privately relieved when the
> holidays end. But that's sad and quite sobering.

For numerous souls, the holidays are not at all sober-
ing—literally—for their search for meaning and merriment
is drowned out in liquor. Business figures reveal that alcohol sales quadruple the last two weeks of December. Other
statistics show more people are killed or maimed by drunk
drivers during holidays. For families affected by alcohol
abuse, the holidays are for certain not joyous.

Many families are not just wrecked, they are devastated
by sorrow. My youngest sister and her husband were both

killed in September by a drunk driver only three blocks from their own home. The first Christmas after their tragic deaths was difficult for everyone in our family. Now it is possible to enjoy the spirit of Christmas again; but our experience has made us more aware of the sadness of others who may have lost a loved one shortly before the holidays and how holidays bring back painful memories of deceased loved ones. For instance, consider what this widow says:

> I just dread holidays now because I long for years past when all my family got together. The first Christmas after my husband died was awful. All I could think about was missing him while everybody else was enjoying Christmas with their loved ones.

Coping with Extra Pressures

Scheduling holiday plans poses yet another frustration for many families. Whether to visit one set of parents or the other, when to open gifts, whether or not to buy gifts for certain relatives—and on and on grows the list of decisions to be made.

The increasing number of divorces and remarriages creates burgeoning sets of stepfamilies. Ivan Howard, a family therapist in Thousand Oaks, California, and president of the Stepfamily Association of America, admits that in stepfamilies conflicts over holiday preparations and plans can break out between "a whole cast of characters, including ex-spouses and in-laws from the previous marriages." Stepfamilies might also, this expert adds, "find themselves going over the river, through the woods and across twenty states to visit the gallimaufry of grandmothers."[3]

"Bah! Humbug!" Many seem to be repeating the words of Ebeneezer Scrooge in Charles Dickens's *A Christmas Carol* as they join the swelling ranks of those who say that materialism has infested the spirit of Christmas. The authors of *Unplug the Christmas Machine* observe, "Children can end up not appreciating their gifts because they get too many of them."

Some women, so it seems, "feel an extraordinary responsibility to make the holidays a wonderful experience for
everyone, to construct the kinds of celebrations we see in
women's magazines. They don't feel they're getting anything out of the experience unless they're exhausted."
And in the end, trying to keep up with all the gift-giving,
party-going, and tradition-keeping is not only unimportant,
but can actually get in the way of what people really want:
to feel in touch with the people they love.

Setting Priorities

What can be done as a rebuttal against all these misguided and materialistic monsters that seem to be choking
out the joy in Christmas, as well as other holidays? How can
we restore some of the real—or perceived—sparkle of yesteryear? Consider what the authors of *Let's Make a Memory*
have to say:

> We believe that special moments don't just happen: they
> have to be planned on purpose! In this hectic world when
> the pace at which we all live is so frantic, we as families
> must make a covenant with each other to make time for
> simple things.[4]

First, we need to remind ourselves what Christmas—or
any holiday—is all about. A brief account of an episode in
the life of Christ, whose birthday is the reason we celebrate
Christmas, provides some insight. It involves Martha and
Mary, and is recorded in Luke 10:38–42:

> As Jesus and the disciples continued on their way to
> Jerusalem they came to a village where a woman named
> Martha . . . the jittery type, . . . was worrying about
> the big dinner she was preparing. She came to Jesus and
> said, ". . . doesn't it seem unfair to you that my sister just
> sits here [listening to you] while I do all the work? Tell her
> to come and help me." But the Lord said to her, "Martha,
> dear friend, you are so upset over all these details! There is

really only one thing worth being concerned about. Mary has discovered it . . ." (TLB).

This simple incident illustrates a profound truth—truly a great lesson in priority setting—that listening at the feet of Jesus as Mary did—or putting *relationships* back into Christmas—is much more important than all the frenzied activities we suffer at holiday time.

Most of us would agree with this in theory. But how do we break away from the Martha-type and become more the Mary-type—the type who puts people and relationships before all the hustle and bustle? Consider the following ways to lessen the stress on your marriage at holiday time and bring your family closer together:

1. *Talk over your concern with your marriage partner and other family members.* Explore what you want out of the holiday. Then relay your conclusion to others who will be affected by your decision. A letter to Ann Landers summarizes a situation evidently faced by many:

Dear Ann: For the past 31 years I have had my brother and his whole family for Thanksgiving dinner, Christmas dinner and Easter brunch.

We love him and his wife dearly, and their children and grandchildren are all wonderful, but I would consider it heaven to be a guest once in a while.

How can I call a halt after all this time without offending anyone? It was my husband's idea to write to you.
Milwaukee Dilemma

Dear Milwaukee: Family traditions die hard—especially when good ol' "Aunt Nell" sets a great table and is such a lovely hostess.

Phone your brother's wife today and tell her that you want to alternate from now on and that you'd like the next holiday dinner to be at her home. It's as simple as that.[5]

2. *Discuss with each other how much money you are going to spend on gifts, and then decide on a portion of that to give to*

some worthy cause. Several years ago at Christmas a friend of mine had her heart set on some beautiful country-blue cookware. As Christmas approached she read in a magazine how a contribution of a few cents a day would feed a starving child in a drought-plagued African country. "That's about the same amount the country-blue cookware costs," she thought to herself. Her desire for that cookware melted away as she clipped out that page in the magazine and made out a check.

Seeing his wife's childlike glee, the husband made a similar decision. He had been struggling to lose weight, but the pounds stayed on as tenaciously as did his habit of visiting the candy machine every afternoon at break time. He made a photostatic copy of the magazine page, and rigged up a clear plastic container with the page inside it. Each time he looked at the container on his desk, he looked squarely in the eyes of the child. Every afternoon at break time he would look at the child's face and promptly put his change in this container rather than in the candy machine. He lost some weight, a hungry child was fed, and his heart was filled—not only at Christmas, but all through the year.

3. *Give a gift of time to someone.* Helping someone should not be limited to certain holidays, but perhaps holidays add an extra incentive to find ways to help others. I was touched by the account of one family in our church. The husband is a physician, so time with his own family is limited. Nevertheless, he and his wife and their three school-age daughters help serve Thanksgiving and Christmas dinner to the poor in our local Salvation Army program.

Here's how two brothers beat the holiday blues:

> I had just broken up with my fiancée, my 34-year-old brother Mike had just broken up with his wife, and Christmas 1983 was not shaping up to be one of the merrier ones on record. So what did we do?
> Mike rented a Santa Claus suit, I bought a red stocking cap with a fluffy white ball at the end and the name "Elmo" monogrammed on it, and together we drove off to visit the residents of Bradbury Nursing Home in Belfast,

Maine. . . . It was time to turn into Santa and his hitherto-unknown elf, Elmo.

I pulled out my Guild guitar, tuned it up after not playing it for a year and together we marched in the front door. "O, you better not cry, you better not pout, you better not shout I'm telling you why. . . ." The words got mixed up, but we were not to be stopped by mere details.

About 50 residents awaited us, sitting in the community room. All were old, most sat in wheelchairs, and some knew the words to our songs better than we did. One lovely lady even danced. "Don't you know the words to these songs?" asked another. We had a good laugh over my lousy singing.

Then it was time to visit the men and women who couldn't leave their rooms. Some had no idea who we were or what we were doing there. Others smiled radiantly, clutched my hand, and thanked me for coming. "My son is in Texas," said one old man. "He can't take off to visit his father."

When it came time to leave, the short gift of time we had given them seemed so inadequate. . . . I've returned almost every year since with Mike, finding again each time the true spirit of the season, and the gumption of Elmo the Elf.[6]

4. *Do something as a couple for someone who will never know who did it.* Doing something for someone without thought of that person doing something for you in return is a gift to the giver, as well as the recipient. Carrying out some generous gesture together has a mysterious bonding effect. For example, when an elderly couple went to the doctor each week, their neighbors raked their leaves and left a load of their favorite kind of firewood. Every time the younger couple thought about their surprise gift, they felt a warm glow even more satisfying and lasting than that given by the firewood they provided.

5. *Give a gift of gratitude.* Between now and the next major holiday take just a few minutes and share just one thing a day with your mate for which you are grateful. Sometimes share verbally, and sometimes surprise each other with notes. However you relate your gift of gratitude, it will put a

lilt into both your lives. One Proverb puts it this way: "Like apples of gold in settings of silver/Is a word spoken in right circumstances" (Prov. 25:11, NASB).

Are holidays joyous times that bring family members closer to each other? Frankly, to paraphrase Charles Dickens:

> *They can be the best of times or the worst of times. It all depends on you!*

MYTH 13:

High Standards Create Highly Satisfying Marriages

WHILE ON AN ASSIGNMENT in Rabat and Casa Blanca, Morocco, I found the Moroccan people intriguing. I was fascinated by the patterns they weave into their rugs. They make imperfections in the rugs on purpose because they consider only God as perfect, and to assume to make a "perfect" rug would be presumptuous—if not blasphemous.

If only marriage partners would take a lesson from those wise Moroccan rug weavers! Logic infers that people with high standards create highly satisfying marriages. Not so. Paradoxical as it may seem, those who set extremely high standards for themselves and their marriage are courting disaster.

Why Good Marriages Fail

Human experience is full of such ironies. The high divorce rate today, for example, would suggest that marriages are not as good as they used to be when divorce was less epidemic. "This is not altogether true," points out a twice-divorced individual now in a satisfying marriage in its tenth year. "We expect so much more of marriage now. When marriage fails to live up to those grandiose expectations, it is considered a failure." As impossible as it may sound, says Dr. Richard Farson, author of an article describing "Why Good Marriages Fail," good marriages probably fail more often than bad ones. "What's more," contends this expert, "they fail precisely because they *are* good."[1]

The higher the expectations, the greater the dissatisfaction and disappointment when the marriage partners find they cannot live up to them. Furthermore, the closer the partners approach the "perfect" marriage, the less tolerant they are of any imperfection that creeps in. They begin to snip here and there at little knots, tangles, or ravelled edges, trying to preserve their "ideal" marriage. At other times they cut large swaths in the marriage relationship with their scissor-sharp censure. Most of the time they try to exert complete control.

One of my relatives was married for seven years to a perfectionist who made life miserable for everyone. Says my relative: "Those who set extremely high standards cannot tolerate loose ends or frayed edges in themselves, their mate, or in the marital relationship."

The tensile strength of most marriages cannot survive the strong, steady tugging and tearing, the push and pull, and the critique and criticism of perfectionists. One victim of a marriage of two perfectionists summarized what frequently happens when expectations are unrealistically high: "The higher the standards, the harder the fall."

But the other extreme is also best avoided. Thus, I also don't advocate following the advice of the English poet and satirist Alexander Pope, who said, "Blessed is he who expects nothing, for he shall never be disappointed." Marriage partners need some dreams or goals to work for in their marriage. A marriage with no aspirations would crumble like a stone wall stuck together with paper paste. But the other extreme, that of the precipitous push for perfection, also is disastrous, as highlighted by English poet Robert Browning: "What's come to *perfection* perishes."

A Little Knowledge Is a Dangerous Thing

The more couples learn through books, counseling, or marriage workshops about marriage and how it "ought to be," the higher their expectations grow for their own marriage. Too often, however, expectations are so high that they can't possibly be met, so failure is inevitable. Don't get me wrong. These efforts to improve marriage are not necessarily bad, in fact they are usually good, but they can also give people the feeling that they are in complete charge of their lives, that problems are basically of their own making, and that the solutions are within their control. This is simply not true. Here is one married person's comment on this:

> Perhaps if we as humans were perfect, this would be true. But we are not perfect, and the situations in which we find ourselves are not perfect; and the control we can initiate over ourselves, others, and the situation is often grossly overrated.

Thus, the saying, "A little knowledge is a dangerous thing," takes on new meaning as applied to marriage. The more we learn about what a marriage relationship might be like, the wider the disparity grows between what we want and what we are capable of achieving.

Anything Worth Doing Is Worth Doing Well

Perfectionists take to heart and apply to every facet of their lives such familiar sayings as, "If you are going to do it, do it right." A good friend described this approach to life this way:

> We compare, contrast, compete, contest. We examine, evaluate, exert, excel. We regiment, rival, race, rate. We strive, succeed, surpass, set records.

Americans have become especially proficient as perfectionists in our pursuits of leisure and relaxation. We push, press, participate, persevere—and try to be perfect. We play tennis and racquetball to win. We buy a house with a lawn so we can get outdoors to loosen up and slacken our pace. Then we wind up worrying, mowing, trimming, fertilizing, watering, mulching, aerating—and worrying even more.

We condense marathon activities into our vacations and squeeze countless scenes into our sightseeing schedule. We visit as many national shrines as we can in the shortest possible time so that even time-management experts marvel at our efficiency. If yesterday we jogged two miles, today we will go for three, and tomorrow, four.

In an article entitled "'All-or-nothing' Outlook Harmful," a psychologist says many of us are products of a society that told its children of yesteryear, "If you can't do something well, don't do it at all."[2] And that is exactly the attitude applied today toward marriage. Impossible goals are set and couples strain compulsively to reach them. Even a 99 percent success rate is seen as failure by people with an "all-or-nothing" outlook. This mindset is why many people divorce: If they cannot have a perfect marriage, they will not have one at all.

The Perfectionists' Locked-Tight Personality

Individuals who set unrealistically high standards for their marriage often have a "locked-tight" personality. They live in an airtight cell, dwarfing and starving their own personality and that of their mate by not allowing enough spontaneity—sunshine and happiness. Here is how one wife describes her perfectionistic husband:

> He lives life with one foot on the brake; he lives in fear of doing or saying the wrong thing. He is painfully constricted, compulsive, and inhibited. Oh, how I have wished he would just relax and quit telling me how to do *everything*—even things that don't really matter, like how to hang my towel on the rack so it'll dry faster, how to arrange the things in the refrigerator so they'll be easier to reach, and how to fold the newspapers before putting them into the waste container.

Often reared with a strong work ethic, perfectionists tend to let "getting things done" and getting them done *their way* take precedence over the emotion-sharing that all relationships need to grow and flourish. Psychologist Harold LeCrone points out that perfectionists often set priorities in which "things and other people" become more important than the marriage relationship, and "commitment to each other and their marriage becomes an idealistic dream instead of the foundation of their relationship."[3]

In a marriage enrichment workshop Del and I attended, Tim LaHaye analyzed people's behavior by categorizing their personalities as primarily choleric, sanguine, melancholy, or phlegmatic. LaHaye says perfectionists are usually cholerics who are strong willed, determined, independent, visionary, productive, decisive, and confident. They are usually the individuals we consider "successful"; they are the ones who "bite off more than they can chew—and then chew it."

The negative side of choleric-perfectionists, LaHaye pointed out, is they are unemotional or cold, self-sufficient, impetuous, proud, domineering, inconsiderate, unforgiving, and sarcastic. They often are more concerned with "being right" than with how others feel; they rely heavily on logic and "common sense" rather than upon people's feelings. They have difficulty admitting making a mistake; they can hardly ever apologize—rarely uttering the words, "I'm sorry. I goofed!" They cannot comprehend how their cold, calculating comments could possibly hurt another's feelings. And as the wife of one perfectionist put it, they are "as stubborn as a new bottle of ketchup."

Dr. James Dobson suggests in *Straight Talk to Men and Their Wives* that perfectionism causes dissatisfaction, and that in about 90 percent of the divorces he has studied he has found "an extremely busy husband who is in love with his work and who tends to be somewhat insensitive, unromantic, and noncommunicative, married to a lovely, vulnerable, romantic woman who has severe doubts about her worth as a human being. They become a matched team: he works like a horse and she nags."[4]

Women can also be perfectionists, and they are not without their problems. A friend, Jackie Toby, told me about an article in which she read that women executives have a significantly higher suicide rate than other women in different roles. I admit to being a perfectionist (I have, of course, more of the good traits of a choleric than all those bad traits!), and I hold a demanding executive position in a large international company. So I was particularly interested in this article; of course, I take most research findings with a grain of salt—also a true sign of a cynical choleric. But I know personally that being a perfectionist in a demanding position and at the same time wanting to be a perfect wife and mother can create pressure to the boiling point.

Some perfectionists cope by trying to make everyone else as perfect as they are. They are the "picture straighteners on the wall of life." Someone once said that perfectionists are always giving others a piece of their mind when they actually need every piece of it themselves. Chuck Swindoll also offers commentary on this kind of people; he says they may not tell people off, but they sure find it easy to freeze people out with their judgmental spirit, intolerance, cynicism, condemning attitude, unapproachability, and so on. He describes such treatment as part of the perfectionist's "whip routine." "Whips like these," emphasizes Swindoll, "will beat you to death, like scourges in your side." They can also kill a good marriage.[5]

When Your Best Is Not Good Enough

In an article entitled "The Ideal Relationship and Other Myths about Marriage," the author says he has often wished for the courage to preach a wedding sermon called "Marriage Is Not the Greatest." The perfect time to preach it would be before the last notes of "O Perfect Love" have faded into the hush of the candlelit sanctuary and before the misty bridal veil has been raised for the groom's kiss. He explains:

Family-oriented magazines publish article after article of advice on improving bliss. But despite the seemingly limitless

how-to's, marriage today seems more fragile than ever . . .
society and the church have a faulty view of it . . . most
laud a romantic image of marriage as life's ultimate source of
true joy.[6]

Any marriage measured against the faulty yardstick of
total joy, emphasizes this author, will fall short because
every marriage faces conflict, smashed fantasies, and
bruised egos.

Marriages may also crumble—or suffer from bouts of
temporary disenchantment—because the partners feel
compelled to present a facade to others. They want others
to think their marriage is "successful," partly because they
think the marriages of others are successful. The truth is
none of us really knows what the marriages of our friends
are like because they have shown us only the aspects of
their marriage that they want us to see. And those aspects,
of course, are the best aspects, for we have been conditioned since childhood to put our best foot forward.

Marriages of religious individuals may suffer special disappointment, for these spouses are often taught that their
unions will be better than those in which God is neither
recognized as the head of the relationship nor provides
divine guidance. These marriages may be better; but they
still are not *perfect,* and the marriage partners are shocked
into despair when they discover this painful reality. One of
my friends attending a church-sponsored marriage enrichment weekend summarized the despondency she suffered
when she realized that her God-ordained marriage was not
perfect:

> My husband and I did all the "right" things, and yet we still
> clashed and at times felt like failures. We felt like our best
> was never good enough.

Partners who set unrealistically high standards expect
someday to be completely happy, to reach an ultimate goal.
If a couple is to achieve fulfillment within marriage, the
illusive dream of "the perfect marriage" must fade. Here is
one marriage partner's observation:

It took a long time, and a lot of hurtful—and unnecessary—disappointments before I realized that "the perfect marriage" is a fallacy, not a fact. Expecting to be a fugitive from the law of averages and to create the perfect marriage forced me for a long time to live in the future—which would never come—rather than in the imperfect present. When I finally accepted the fact that even quite godly people who are living very good lives will have some ups and downs . . . well, frankly, a great load was lifted, and our marriage started to become much more comfortable and enjoyable.

Fulfilling Marital Roles Generates Dissatisfaction

As ironic as it sounds, sometimes fulfilling society's high-standard role expectations as men and women can actually breed discontent because these roles are so limiting and yet so demanding. You would think that a woman who is successful at being feminine, understanding, kind, emotional, and yielding would be the perfect partner for a man who is masculine, logical, assertive, and a strong leader. Unfortunately, life is simply not that simple. The women's movement helped us see the oppressive concept of "woman's role" and "woman's place." Now men are more openly expressing dissatisfaction with the male macho stereotype that leads to overwhelming feelings of pressure to perform and to produce.

In an article called "Male Mystique" an intriguing book was highlighted—*Quiet Desperation: The Truth about Successful Men.* In this book the results of interviews with 4,126 men revealed that about half the men in middle management positions said their lives seemed "empty and meaningless" despite years spent striving to achieve their professional goals. Nearly 70 percent of the senior executives said they had neglected their families in the pursuit of their professional goals, and half of these highly successful executives said that if they could start all over again they would spend less time working and more time with their wives and children. Nearly 60 percent of the high achievers felt they had "sacrificed their identities and wasted years of their lives pursuing material rewards."[7]

There is a lot of evidence that men are breaking out of their corporate and personal straitjackets; they are questioning their roles, reevaluating their career goals, altering their lifestyles and redefining their personal relationships. For so long they set high standards for their careers, only to feel betrayed by the system to which they gave their hearts and souls. Says one former business executive:

> I set high standards for myself in my career, and I met them. I thought being successful in my career would automatically make me a successful husband and father. Boy, was I wrong!
>
> When my company was sold, I was forced to retire early. The new company didn't need me, but neither did my wife and kids. After all, my family had learned to live without me all those years I was giving my heart and soul to my career. Of course, I often excused my absenteeism as a husband and father by telling my family, "I'm doing this for all of you." If I had it to do all over again, I'd sure not get on the materialism merry-go-round again.

Ideally, the intimacy and the security of marriage should provide respite from society's materialistic and artificial yardstick of success. Unfortunately, many husbands and wives say they cannot let down in marriage either because marriage serves not as a buffer against the impositions of society but as a reinforcer. Marriage partners themselves, in fact, force these roles on each other. Then the inability to live up to the high standards set by mates makes matters even worse. Kari, an executive with a large accounting firm, comments:

> My husband is supportive of my career and offers sincere encouragement, but he also expects me to excel in the role of wife and mother. He denies it, but he puts pressure on me in subtle little ways.

Here is the husband's rebuttal to Kari's accusations:

> Kari actually puts more pressure on herself than I do. She sets high standards in everything she does, and, of course,

she is frustrated when she falls short of being the perfect career woman, the perfect wife, and the perfect mother. I simply think she perceives that I expect her to fill all these roles in a superhuman way. She could say the same about me. We wind up frustrated, blaming each other for the pressure to perform perfectly in our various roles, when it actually is the society we live in.

The Better Marriage Gets, the Better It Has to Be

Even marriage partners who rise above—or get around—the stifling husband-wife stereotypes suffer frustration because once the basic needs of the marriage have been satisfied, the partners move on to higher-order needs. By human nature, people are restless and never satisfied. Once they have met one level of needs, according to Abraham Maslow, father of the self-actualization movement, they yearn to move to the next level. They are caught up in an always-accelerating pattern of getting better and better.

The better marriage gets, then, the better we expect it to be. Not only do we expect it to meet all our basic needs but our much higher needs as well. We expect marriage to provide intellectual companionship, warm intimate moments, shared values, deep romantic love, and great sexual pleasures. But then discontent rises precisely because we cannot bear to live with the incongruity between what we are actually experiencing in our marriage and what we have come to believe is possible. So, strange as it seems, it is a myth that people with high standards create highly satisfying marriages.

A blurred snapshot in the album under the television set in our family room brings into sharp focus for me the dangers of striving too hard for high standards in marriage.

Once when I was flying from Cyprus to Dar es Salaam, Tanzania, the pilot announced that we would soon be passing Mount Kilimanjaro. Camera in hand, I peered through the dense clouds; in a fleeting but majestic moment the clouds parted and a brilliant sunray spotlighted the western mountaintop, and I got my treasured snapshot. Years before, I had read Ernest Hemingway's story, "The Snows of Kilimanjaro," and these captivating words:

> Kilimanjaro is a snow covered mountain 19,710 feet high and is said to be the highest mountain in Africa. Its western summit is called the Masai "Ngaje Ngai," the House of God. Close to the western summit there is the dried and frozen carcass of a leopard. No one has explained what the leopard was seeking at that altitude.

There is a dark spot in my snapshot of Kilimanjaro, and I imagine that it is that well-meaning but dead leopard. My snapshot reminds me of the danger lying in wait for marriage partners who, like the leopard, strive too hard, climb *too* high. Why can't we be satisfied to climb high, but not too high? Why can't we profit from the wisdom of the Moroccan rug weavers and be satisfied with a less-than-perfect marriage, recognizing that . . . only God is perfect.

MYTH 14:

Hard Times Bring Marriage Partners Closer Together

Marti picked up her husband Dave from work. Then they both picked up their only child, Lisa, from kindergarten and ate lunch with her. They drove Dave back to his job, and then Marti and Lisa went to the post office to meet Lisa's baby-sitter for the afternoon. Marti gave a friendly wave to the baby-sitter while Lisa hopped out on the passenger's side—failing to slam the heavy door hard enough to close it well. When Marti saw her little daughter go in front of the truck and toward the baby-sitter's car, she leaned over to shut the door more securely. Sitting upright, Marti noted the way was clear, shifted gears, and pulled forward. "I felt a thump," Marti later said—which turned out to be Lisa, who had dropped a toy in front of the truck and gone back to get it. Marti, the devoted mother, had run over and killed her own daughter. [1]

Accidentally killing someone, especially your own child, creates one of the hardest times a marriage will ever undergo. My university research on "Families in Crises" observed this in family after family. I also saw how this particular calamity and other tragedies often tear marriages apart rather than bringing the partners closer together. Dave and Marti, for instance, had enjoyed an idyllic marriage; but after Lisa's death, despair and other heart-wrenching emotions nearly destroyed that marriage.

Romanticizing about past eras and how families clung together in hard times has only reinforced our belief in this myth. Hard times may have forged families together in days gone by, when divorce was not as frequently considered as an option. But many members from broken families in my research claim a crisis or a series of problems accounted for the wrecking of their marriage. Divorce was often precipitated by a crisis, such as one of the partners accidentally killing someone in a car wreck, financial turmoil caused by such events as the husband losing his job, a teen-ager's using drugs, serious illness or disability of one of the marriage partners, the children, or an elderly parent, or one of the family members drinking chronically and excessively.

Ideally, family members pull together, giving each other consolation and encouragement when hard times hit, but this is often not the case. Instead, marriage partners are frequently wrought with extreme feelings of failure, disgrace, guilt, bitterness, and even physical violence. These feelings can culminate in divorce because, as one person in my research put it, "Many marriage partners simply find it easier to flee than to stay and fight the overwhelming circumstances and emotions tragedies generate."

What Makes the Difference?

Why are some marriages destroyed by a crisis while other couples work through it? Suffering and tragedy seem to have contributed to the greatness of some individuals, such as Abraham Lincoln, who survived numerous heartbreaking losses, including the death of his mother and two of his own children. He gave this advice to anyone having great problems: "When you come to the end of your rope . . . tie a knot and hang on." Here are some specific ways and qualities others have found helpful in surviving hard times in their marriage. When you are "at the end of your rope," these suggestions may also help you "tie a knot and hang on."

Survivors Are Prepared

Marriage partners who grow closer together *through* a crisis generally are more prepared *before* the crisis. Preparation may involve financial readiness either through insurance or savings. Preparation may also be the ability to communicate openly and effectively, being able to talk about problems and work through them to possible solutions. If two partners cannot talk honestly and constructively when things are going smoothly in the marriage, they are almost doomed to have trouble communicating when the going gets rough. Learning to share feelings openly, to encourage one another, to avoid accusations and finger-pointing, and to "pull together" is one of the most important preparations a couple can make for working their way through the inevitable ups and downs all marriages experience.

Another important facet of preparation has to do with attitude. Families who survive misfortunes usually are those who take the initiative. When problems do come, they take purposeful action. They do not see themselves as simply reactors in society, being at the mercy of happenstance. They make things happen. Gerry and Helen's "let's-do-something" attitude has helped their marriage from the very beginning. Consider Helen's analysis:

> We have always taken decisive steps to improve our marriage. At first we were caught up in our careers, but we soon realized we were drifting apart. We started spending ten or twenty minutes after the meal just talking. During the meal we tried to include the kids and have good "family time," but then we'd let the kids watch TV or do homework. It was amazing how just a few quality minutes a day helped strengthen our interest in each other. Then when our youngest son was hit by a car while riding his bike and was in ICU for three days and required a lot of medical attention afterward, we already knew how to

communicate with each other. In addition, we had built strong emotional reserves and positive attitudes so we could rally around each other to do whatever it took to survive the hard times and make the best of the situation.

Preparation is summarized by an ancient Chinese proverb that instructs, "Dig the well *before* you thirst!"

You Gotta Have Perspective

Marriage partners from all walks of life suffer cruel blows, and all experience frustration, bitter disappointments, and failures from time to time. Some marriages crumble under the weight of catastrophe, while other spouses put the shattered pieces of their lives back together; their marriage is strengthened as they turn tragedies into triumphs and become victors instead of victims.

How marriage partners react to trouble may vary at different ages and according to their understanding of the threat. Personality and attitudes, as well as past experiences, may also influence how they react toward events in their lives. The late, great Harvard psychologist William James pointed out what he considered to make the difference from the very beginning: "Acceptance of what has happened is the first step in overcoming the consequences of any misfortune."

When a marriage is afflicted by some misfortune, the partners who are brought closer together as they struggle through it are those who realize they have not been singled out by some cosmic lottery. They simply recognize a fact expressed well in Charles Dickens's *David Copperfield:* "Accidents will occur in the best regulated families." When the partners realize *everyone* has trials, tribulations, and tragedies sooner or later, then they are assuming the kind of attitude that will help them get out of their quagmire.

In a similar vein, people need to understand fully that neither troubles nor tragedies are necessarily punishment from God. It is a fact of life that hard times also strike godly people. To survive calamity with sanity intact and to

prevent it from wrecking the marriage, spouses must come
to the same conclusion about God and tragedy that Rabbi
Harold Kushner did in his book, *When Bad Things Happen to
Good People.* " . . . He makes His sun to rise on the evil and
the good and He pours rain upon the just and the unjust"
(Matt. 5:45, MLB). One husband who had suffered more
than his share of misfortunes summarized this quality that
is so essential to survival: "You gotta have perspective."

An Attitude of Gratitude

Couples who make hard times work for their marriage
not only emphasize their positive feelings toward each
other, they downplay or de-emphasize their negative ones.
They also avoid using each other as a scapegoat. When the
Johnsons' teen-age son, their middle child, committed suicide, the entire family was shocked and devastated. Conflict had been constant between father and son. Susan
Johnson comments:

> I was angry at myself for not realizing that things were so
> bad between my husband and our son. But most of all, I
> was angry at my husband. He'd always pushed Tim. From
> the very beginning it seemed like they were determined to
> resist each other. I tried to get my husband to slack up, and
> I tried to get Tim to try just a little more to please his dad.
> And now this. I knew all along that my husband loved
> Tim—and I could see after Tim's suicide that my husband
> was just about to lose his mind. I simply could not continue
> my anger; he never meant for this to happen. I had lost a
> son, but I knew there was no reason to lose a marriage, too.
> And, of course, our other kids needed us more than ever.

As in the case of the Johnsons, when something bad happens, most of us instinctively look for someone to hold responsible. And regardless of the circumstances, it is your
spouse who is likely to be standing right in your line of
vision. But finding fault, placing blame, accusing, and pointing a finger never help—and usually hurt. In the *Reader's
Digest* article, "Make Hard Times Work for Your Marriage,"

psychiatrist Frank Pittman says, "There's no way to win against your spouse. You both win or you both lose."[2]

This same article points out that many experts think it helps for couples to think of the problem—cancer, for example—as something outside their relationship, sort of like a third party they can gang up on. "Instead of saying 'my' cancer, they talk about 'the' cancer," says family therapist William J. Doherty. "Then they can feel united against a common enemy." In addition, expressing gratitude for each other's efforts against the crisis-producing event, circumstances, or conditions helps draw the two marriage partners closer together.

Survivors Talk about Their Problems

Comfortable communication is part of the glue that binds family members together. Open, non-threatening expression of feelings becomes even more essential when troubles develop. Yet too many times couples react to problems with denial and grim stoicism.

In Morton Hunt's article called "Is *Your* Family Crisis-Proof?" some helpful generalizations for any crisis are illustrated from the experience of families who have lost a baby to Sudden Infant Death Syndrome, the unexplained crib death that takes about 5,000 lives every year. Morton describes the work of social scientist John DeFrain, who interviewed over 100 such families. DeFrain says that some families' reaction to SIDS is to sweep it under the rug. They will say, "We have to put it behind us. We have to stop talking about what happened." Those families do badly. Many members of such families develop emotional disorders, drinking problems, and work difficulties, and quite a few of those marriages end in divorce. On the other hand, there are families that talk and talk—pouring out their feelings, going over and over the details. One might say, for instance, "I just had an idea—tell me if I'm crazy—that if only I'd done such-and-such. . . ." The other will listen, then reassure the first that it would not have made any difference, but that it is not crazy to think such things.

Dr. DeFrain emphasizes, "These talkers and listeners re-cover, because they are able to work out a rational expla-nation they can live with, rather than a guilt-produced nightmare."[3]

Open and honest communication laced with tact, appro-priate timing, and acceptance of different ways of perceiv-ing the same problem all seem to be helpful in overcoming a crisis in the family.

Avoid Dwelling on the Past

While it's important to talk about the crisis, it's also im-perative, after a while, to turn your focus away from the past and toward the future. When you have coped with a problem the best way you know how, do not waste time feeling guilty for not having coped better than you did.

Whatever the problem and however or whenever it happens, couples are advised to do the best they can to handle it, not looking back nor dwelling on past mistakes. Instead, they are urged to put the wisdom of the apostle Paul into practice: "Forgetting those things which are be-hind, and reaching forth unto those things which are before . . ." (Phil. 3:13, KJV).

Let Others Help

Turning to other people and to outside organizations for help may be an important buffer when problems beset a marriage. Perhaps because of a stiff-upper-lip independ-ence or fear of being rejected or ostracized, many families keep their problems a secret, trying to manage all by themselves. This puts troubled families at a distinct disad-vantage. Experience of married couples facing problems consistently reveals the ones who seek help from relatives, friends, and support groups ultimately handle the problem more satisfactorily than those who do not.

Professional help has carried many marriages success-fully through devastating events or circumstances. In addi-tion, the burgeoning number of self-help groups forming to assist people with a specific problem attests to the human need for help and encouragement.

Many people have commented that one of the most helpful features of my book, *Because You Care: Practical Ideas for Helping Those Who Grieve,* is its comprehensive list and description of organizations to help people cope with the death of a loved one.[4] Included in this list, for example, is Make Today Count, an organization for helping families cope with the terminal illness of one of its members. Also included is Compassionate Friends. With chapters all over the United States, this organization helps parents of all ages cope with the death of a child—considered by many to be the most heartwrenching loss anyone ever suffers. Other groups help people with problems such as drug addiction, obsessive gambling, or abusive and violent behavior—all problems which can destroy a marriage.

Getting professional help is based on the premise that people should not have to struggle through crises alone—or as a couple. One middle-age father in Atlanta said this about the group for parents whose teen-agers were in a drug-abuse program: "Going to these meetings helped . . . those other men knew what it was like. I knew they understood what I was going through. Professional help saved our marriage."

Finding Grounds for Hope

Couples who survive tragedies generally have a basic optimism that dispels hopelessness. They recognize that most crises have multiple parts, and they know that solving each facet or part of the problem individually probably will be more successful than trying to solve all of them at once.

Even when a problem is permanent, such as the husband or wife being confined to a wheelchair because of an accident or a child having a chronic disease, it is essential to define the situation in positive terms and to concentrate on what can be done. It doesn't help to freeze attention and energies on what cannot be done. Couples who make the best of a bad situation live out the philosophy of the motto

of the Christopher Society: "It's better to light candles than
to curse the darkness."

The Chinese were perhaps the first to recognize the dual
nature of a crisis. Their word for crisis is made with two
characters, one meaning *danger* and one *opportunity.* A crisis
is, in fact, more than just a problem—it is a turning point, a
catalyst which disrupts old behavior patterns, evokes new
responses, and becomes a forceful determinant for new directions and new beginnings. When disaster strikes, marriages that survive deal with it because the partners for
the most part see the positives, not the negatives. They find
grounds for hope, as expressed in this familiar rhyme:

> Two look out through
> the same bars:
> One sees the mud and one
> the stars.

Use Spiritual Resources

Many people claim that their grounds for hope and
source of optimism is a belief in God which gives them a
sense of purpose and strength. Says one woman whose only
son was killed in Vietnam and only daughter died a drug-
related death, "Without a belief that God would help us
survive these awful losses my husband and I would've simply lost our minds." Other grief-stricken couples suffering
similar sorrows agree that a strong religious orientation
with its emphasis on hope, love, and reliance on a Supreme
Being generally is helpful in contending with otherwise
insurmountable problems. One husband elaborated: "An
awareness of God's presence helped us be more patient
with each other, more forgiving, quicker to get over anger,
more positive, and more supportive of each other."

Others who have survived some of life's cruelest blows
contend that God delivers what He promises. Here are
some of the commitments God has kept with people in their
darkest days:

For God has said, "I will never, *never* fail you nor forsake
you" (Heb. 13:5, TLB).
This hope we have as an anchor of the soul, a *hope* both
sure and steadfast . . . (Heb. 6:19, NASB).
God is our refuge and strength, a very present help in
trouble (Ps. 46:1, KJV).
Cast your burden on the Lord, and he shall sustain you
(Ps. 55:22, RSV).

And the most familiar promise of them all is found in the
Twenty-third Psalm:

Yea, though I walk through the valley of the shadow of
death, I will fear no evil: for thou art with me (KJV).

One of the reasons a belief in God is so sustaining is that
such a belief and faith provide a peace of mind in the midst
of chaotic circumstances. It's the peace that Paul promised
to the Philippians that people want for their very own:
"And the peace of God, which passes all understanding . . ." (Phil. 4:7, RSV).

Strong at the Broken Places

Ernest Hemingway wrote, "Life breaks us all and after-
wards many are strong at the broken places." While many
marriages fail after a crisis, those marriage partners who
have survived catastrophies often say in retrospect, "We are
stronger now." Marti said several years after Lisa's tragic
death, "We will never get over Lisa's death; but at least
we can now live with some joy . . . and we now feel like
we can handle anything else that happens to us." Just
like Marti and her husband, numerous other couples speak
about the deep strength that comes from doing whatever it
takes to survive an insufferable blow. They can undoubtedly identify with Viktor Frankl, who, while imprisoned in
a German concentration camp, spoke words of encouragement to the others, referring to Friedrick Nietzche's remark,
"That which does not kill me, makes me stronger."

Tie a Knot and Hang On

The myth that hard times bring marriage partners closer together is not only counterproductive, it is treacherous. Believing that problems *automatically* forge marriage partners together can wreck a marriage. In contrast, like Abraham Lincoln, couples who make a concerted effort to develop positive attitudes and coping skills will more likely be able, when at the end of their rope, to "tie a knot and hang on."

MYTH 15:

Signs of Impending Failure
Are Easy to Detect

ON ONE OF OUR CROSS-country moves I looked through a box marked "mementos." Several wedding invitations from a couple of decades ago caught my attention. Dave and Sara had beautiful invitations and a perfect *wedding* in every detail, but evidently their *marriage* was not so flawless. I heard they divorced after several years of marriage and two children.

Looking over the other wedding invitations, I reminisced about all these long-ago friends. Their wedding days had been filled with joyous thoughts and blissful anticipation of the future. In my mind's eye the picture of Dave and Sara now glared disappointingly different. I envisioned them in a chronic state of dissension, distrust, and distress, each blaming the other and defensively claiming how hard he or she had tried to be loving, to make the marriage a success, to honor their wedding vows, and to prevent the other from sabotaging the effort.

What caused the frightful change? What brought about the startling, heart-stricken metamorphosis for Dave and

Sara while those other couples were enjoying their second or third decades of happy marriage? Were there any warning signs along the way, any signals to alert them to impending dangers? Surely they were not rapturously happy one day and intolerably miserable the next.

As I tried to answer these questions, I began talking to my friends, some happily married, some not. I delved painstakingly back into the reservoir of my own teaching and research on marriage. At last I concluded that there are simply few surefire predictors of marital failure. To be sure, research *has* identified some signs of impending failure, but these are not always present. The first sentence of Tolstoy's *Anna Karenina* expresses an enigmatic message: "Happy families are all alike; every unhappy family is unhappy in its own way."

Common Predictors of Marital Difficulties

Age at marriage is the most reliable predictor of marital stability or instability, as measured by divorce. The younger a couple is at marriage, the more likely their marriage will end in divorce. The marriages of teenagers, for instance, are several times more likely to end in divorce than marriages between older people. Marriages of younger people are more likely to involve premarital pregnancies and financial difficulties. Either one of these factors puts strain on a relationship; when both are present, the marriage is almost doomed from the start.

Warning signs of marital failure have also been associated with *why* someone chooses to marry. Marrying to escape certain circumstances, for instance, may spell future troubles, especially when the factor of escape carries more weight than the relationship with the other person. Getting out of an unpleasant home situation—or a previous bad marriage—is a typical escape factor. Others include escape from a disliked job or the demands of a school program that is not to one's liking.

But back to Dave and Sara. None of these predictors of marital failure seemed to apply. They were twenty-three and twenty-four when they married; they both went away to college. They worked a year after college before marrying. Their first child was born after Dave was well established in his dental practice. Anyone who knew them would have defended their emotional maturity and rationality at the time they got married. So why did their marriage fail?

Continuing my search for reasons, I examined some other premarital considerations. Background factors thought to influence marital happiness and stability include basic personality adjustment, happiness of parents' marriage, relationship with parents, sound socioeconomic surroundings, common goals, interests, values, and expectations, similar attitudes toward sexuality, length of acquaintance and engagement, and parental approval of the marriage.

The idea of the role of basic personality adjustment in marital success—or failure—intrigued me. I found that researchers from the Medical College of Georgia had reported finding that socially nonconforming, impulsive, stimulus-seeking people may be more prone to divorce. "Impulsivity may be associated with the inability to make a strong commitment to somebody," says one of the social psychologists who worked on the study. In addition, this study suggested that individuals who constantly seek stimulation may be more easily bored, which in turn may lead to less tolerance for the everyday routine of maintaining a stable marriage.[1]

An article in *Psychology Today* reported the findings of several studies on divorce. One study suggests that an individual's self-confidence—including a conviction that one is neither inadequate or victimized—is a factor for both men's and women's marital satisfaction. Says psychologist Arlene Skolnick, "Having self-confidence not only makes you happier, it makes your spouse happier, too." In another long-term study, psychologist James J. Conley concluded, "Marital satisfaction was negatively related to neuroticism in both sexes."[2]

Once again I was stumped. The terms *negative, nonconforming, impulsive, stimulus-seeking, inadequate,* or *victimized* simply did not describe the Dave and Sara I knew, and *neurotic* or *hair-triggered* seemed absolutely foreign. I talked to some of our mutual friends, especially those who had kept in closer contact with Dave and Sara. We all concluded that Dave and Sara were the ideal textbook candidates for a happy, enduring marriage.

The Ambiguity of Signposts

Continuing my search for warning signals, I talked to twenty-five divorced individuals; their comments convinced me that marriage breakups are difficult to predict because a warning sign in one relationship may be an acceptable way of life in another, or, strangely enough, it may even denote a strength.

For example, one of my friends who recently celebrated a silver wedding anniversary noted that she and her husband have few common interests. Each spends time pursuing his or her separate hobbies and pastimes. But this has been a positive arrangement for them because, "what time we do spend together is refreshing and enjoyable," she said.

Frequency of sex may also denote marital strength—or weakness! "A desire for sex may indicate a strong bond," maintains Dr. G. B. Dunning, marriage counselor and sex therapist, "but extremely frequent sex may mean *nothing else* exists in the relationship." Continues this psychologist, "If sex is a frantic attempt to seal a relationship void of love, affection, and the enjoyment of non-sexual activities with each other, then the marriage is dangerously fragile and probably will not last."

It is paradoxical that certain behaviors may be warning signs of impending marital failure—or they may signal strength. It simply depends on what the behavior means to each partner.

Real or perceived alternatives available to each partner also influence whether certain signals foreshadow marital disaster. I know one husband and wife who do not even seem to like each other; they argue and say sarcastic things to each other. I simply do not know what holds them together. Both have inherited money, so they could financially afford divorce. But they have stayed together, quarreling and belittling each other for twenty-four years. Perhaps it's because they see no viable alternatives to their situation. Here is what the husband says:

> Nell and I fight all the time. Seems like we don't have much going for us. But she's all I have. I don't know what else I'd do—or where else I'd go. I'd probably be even more miserable without her. She admits she feels the same way. I guess we are an example of that slogan in the old cigarette ad: "I'd rather fight than switch."

In contrast, some partners in a marriage gone sour might find attractive such alternatives as another person with whom the future looks brighter, freedom from the responsibilities of marriage, a new feeling of independence, or the attraction of a new lifestyle.

Why Couples Stay Together

All this information made Dave and Sara's divorce even more of a mystery to me. None of the warning signs of marital disaster could be seen flashing at critical intersections of their marital journey. Why had Dave and Sara's marriage failed? I felt I was getting no closer to an answer—just digging myself deeper and deeper into a hole. Perhaps the way out of this hole is to look at why couples *do* stay together. Then I might be able to see more clearly why others *do not* stay together.

Setting out to discover what happy families had in common, Dolores Curran sent out 500 questionnaires to family professionals—teachers, pastors, social workers, counselors. In her book *Traits of a Healthy Family,* she summarized the traits these professionals had deemed essential for a healthy, lasting marriage.

Their Number One choice was good communication, especially listening. The research participants also said partners in a healthy marriage affirm and support one another; they respect each other and each other's privacy and develop a sense of trust. They share time, rituals, and traditions. They have a sense of play and humor. They exhibit a sense of shared responsibility and value service to others. Even though belonging to the same religious institution was not considered vital, sharing "a strong religious core" was. In addition, the healthy family adhered to "a strong sense of right and wrong." Finally, this research emphasized that the healthy family "admits and seeks help with problems."

In trailblazer research, Nick Stinnett and John DeFrain went directly to marriage partners others had identified as having strong marriages. These two researchers carefully analyzed the responses of 3,000 families and reported their findings in the book *Secrets of Strong Families*. They found that strong families share six major qualities:

1. *Commitment.* They are dedicated to promoting each other's welfare and happiness. They value family unity.

2. *Appreciation.* They show a great deal of appreciation for each other.

3. *Communication.* They have good communication skills and spend a lot of time talking with each other.

4. *Time.* They spend quality time in large quantities with each other.

5. *Spiritual wellness.* They have a sense of greater good or power in life, and this belief gives them strength and purpose.

6. *Coping ability.* They view crises as an opportunity to grow.[3]

These strengths all seemed valid to me, but how was I to know how committed Dave and Sara were to each other and to making their marriage work? How could I even surmise how much appreciation they showed to each other? And how could I measure their spiritual wellness or their coping ability? I was no closer to understanding why a marriage failed when it seemed to have everything going for it.

Why Good Marriages Go Bad

While I was anticipating a trip to visit my mother for her birthday, a friend told me where Sara was living. The city happened to be on the route I would be taking. If Nick Stinnett and John DeFrain and other researchers could visit with complete strangers about some of the most private details of their marriages, why couldn't I visit with a long-time friend and simply ask her, "What happened?"

Telephoning Sara, I explained that I was working on a book and needed her help. She was as gracious and cooperative as I had remembered her, though she did make a perplexing comment in the closing moment of our telephone conversation: "This is not the first book that has been written about me."

Sara and I met at her home. I told her about my search for warning signs of impending marital failure and how I had concluded that none of them seemed characteristic of her and Dave. Then I asked my question: "What happened?" Within ten seconds, the expression on her attractive face changed from little-girl eagerness to pensive thought to a sad but insightful smile. Without a word, she got up from the floral sofa, left the room, and returned with a book in hand. Giving it to me, she said, "Here's the first book that was written about me." The title was *The Drifting Marriage*. And then I read the subtitle: *The Most Common Cause of Marital Failure among Christian Couples*.

"My name is not in the book," Sara said, "and the author has never even heard of me, but this book describes exactly what happened to Dave and me." Taking the book from me, Sara flipped through the pages, stopping on a page with these words underlined:

> Drifting. Not only is it the most common form of marital failure, it is also the most dangerous. It is subtle. It is quiet. It is non-offensive. It sounds no alarms. It just gradually creeps into our lives. And then it destroys.[4]

Not taking her eyes off the book, Sara said softly, "Dave read this book, and he agrees that's what happened to us.

Many others I've talked to say it was true for them." Turning to another page, she commented, "Dave underlined this paragraph:"

> Marital failure is a process—not an act. It is a destination which is journeyed toward—not an initial port of entry. And like most journeys, the process of marital failure requires both time and the taking of many steps. Step by step . . . one irresponsible action followed by another . . . slowly but surely . . . the dreaded destination is approached.[5]

While Sara and I thumbed through the book, I wondered how many of the one million people who are granted a divorce each year in the United States would say exactly what she and Dave said: "This book describes what happened to us."

I wondered how many went through marriage month after month, year after year, with kids, careers, and everything else vying for top priority and prime time while the marriage relationship itself was put on the back burner. When it finally was checked, no warmth was left. Negligence had insidiously, stealthily dissolved all feelings for each other. The two marriage partners had lost their marriage by default. They had drifted irretrievably apart. *They had fallen prey to the dangerous myth that warning signs of impending marital failure are fairly easy to detect.* The words of Edna St. Vincent Millay came rushing to mind: "Tis not love's going hurts my days. But that it went in little ways."

As Sara and I sat in momentary silence, I thought of the qualities of strong marriages: commitment, appreciation, communication, time, spiritual wellness, and coping ability. *Good marriages—those that satisfy and last—require more than merely the absence of dangerous threats,* I told myself. *A happy marriage requires time, attention, nurturance.*

Going Home

Interrupting the silence, Sara said, "I have to pick up Lisa from school . . . Want to ride along?" I hastily explained that I had several hours left to drive and that my mother would have dinner waiting. We both agreed we wanted to visit again soon.

After leaving Sara's, I stopped at the first public phone I saw and called Del. Waiting eagerly for him to answer the phone, I said aloud, "Drifting apart is a tragic waste, a painful, pointless way to lose a good marriage." When my husband finally answered, I blurted, "Del, I love you and I'm glad you're my husband . . . I'll be home a few days early."

MYTH 16:

Divorce Lets You Begin a Fresh New Life

FEELING TRAPPED in a marriage gone sour, many spouses daydream about a new life "AD"—After Divorce. They see themselves living a relaxed, carefree lifestyle, answering to no one but themselves, and relieved of the overwhelming financial responsibilities that somehow piled up during their marriage.

If they could just break away, get out from under the pressures, the bickering, the monotony, and the hopelessness of the failed marriage, they could wipe the slate clean, start all over—and begin a fresh, new life.

If they could just get the children away from the other spouse, some parents think, they would all be much happier.

Other discontented spouses find themselves drawn from one marriage into another. The new one, they believe, will be strong where the other was weak.

Sometimes it does happen this way. Divorced people do find happiness. But they don't really start a fresh, new life. They carry along with them forever the scars of what they left behind. And sometimes those scars run painfully deep.

Countless divorced people describe how, after their marriages broke up, they merely exchanged one set of problems for another, ranging from financial pressures and child custody to property disputes and a perplexing complexity of relating to children, other relatives (including former in-laws), friends (especially couples), other church members, and business associates. A relative of mine who was going through a divorce describes what often happens:

> Friends who used to call or chat when we'd meet at the shopping mall quit calling and cut short their conversations when we'd see each other. I felt so deserted. I guess they felt they didn't know what to say. Or perhaps they thought I preferred not to be reminded of the divorce. People didn't have to say anything about the divorce, but they didn't seem to want to even be around me or to talk about anything.

Like my relative, many other divorcing individuals admit suffering from increased feelings of failure, rejection, humiliation, guilt, anger, and isolation. Here is another person's description:

> In the most practical terms, divorce is like a forest fire that ravages an entire countryside. It burns down what's in front of it and leaves behind an ugliness and vulnerability, a sense in all concerned of being violated. In a divorce, it doesn't matter whether you are the one who started the fire or whether you just got caught in the middle of it. Whenever a marriage is seared to its roots, no one emerges uninjured.[1]

Divorce, unfortunately, frequently fails to deliver the partners' optimistic expectations for a new life. Regardless of the ultimate outcome, most say they simply were not prepared for all the trials and tribulations encountered throughout the divorce process and its aftermath. The expectation that divorce will provide an opportunity to begin a new life soon shatters and is reduced to false hope and a painful myth.

Divorce Is Not "the End of the End"

One of the most perplexing misconceptions that divorcing couples hold is that divorce is a single event. Because of her long-term research on divorce and the effects of divorce on family members, Judith Wallerstein is considered by some to be the world's foremost expert on the aftermath of divorce. She describes divorce as a chain of events. Divorce involves a series of legal, social, psychological and sexual changes, strung complexly together, spreading out over a longer period of time than most people realize.

All of these changes require adjustments, insists Dr. Wallerstein. She adds, "Change is nearly always stressful even under the best of circumstances." She continues, "When all these changes—changes in neighborhood, in jobs, in schools, in friends, in standard of living . . . the list goes on and on—are forced on individuals by divorce, they are absolutely overwhelming, even for the marriage partner who wanted the divorce in the first place." This researcher points out, "For the marriage partner who did not want the divorce and for the children, who for the most part never want their parents to split up, the adjustments are even more staggering."

Dr. Wallerstein has not only studied divorce but has spent countless hours counseling members of divorced families. She elaborates, "The widening effects of the divorce seem to go on and on. The strong emotions—feelings of rejection, failure and social censure—have an uncanny staying power. They erupt unpredictably about the time you think you have them under control." One of the persons she counseled summed up the feelings of many others by concluding, "There is no painless divorce."[2]

Others share Dr. Wallerstein's belief that divorce is a process, not a one-time event. Here is the way one clergyman describes it:

And the end was not the end. When a marriage detonates, as any divorced person will tell you, the debris lives on; it is not biodegradable. The spouses simply cannot pretend it's a new world and the other partner has left for Saturn. Children, money, holidays, memories, and a dozen other things keep raising their hands for attention.[3]

A divorced man echoed the feeling of many others that the repercussions of divorce go on and on:

I think a death is easier than a divorce, because there's a finality to it. This sort of thing—it goes on.

When she began her study of divorced families, Dr. Wallerstein anticipated ending the study of each family eighteen months after their divorce. She explained, "We figured that the transition would pretty well be made by one and a half years after the divorce. Instead, we found many unresolved issues even at eighteen months after the divorce. Feelings of anger, humiliation, and rejection still ran high in children and parents." Even more surprising, according to Dr. Wallerstein and her co-researcher, was this observation: "We found greater incidences of depression at five years after the divorce than at earlier periods following the divorce."

Some divorcing couples, of course, experience less stress and conflict than others, but even they are not prepared for the stress that accompanies the most amicable of divorces. The emotional turmoil often reduces the ability of divorcees to relate meaningfully with friends and relatives—and even themselves. Concerned and well-meaning people, in turn, frequently do not know how to respond to the divorcees' strong emotions such as anger and hostility. Not only do the non-divorced not know how to relate to the divorced, the divorced often do not understand their own feelings and reactions. A divorced friend's comments are typical:

I found myself overwhelmed at times by a strong mixture of inexplicable feelings. Welling up inside of me, these feelings would explode or gush out as though a gigantic floodgate had opened—always at the most unexpected and inappropriate time. I constantly fought an identity crisis, with inner conflict vacillating between my longing for the

security of marriage to my yearning for an escape from
an intolerable situation that only divorce promised. My
friends never knew how to react to my mercurial moods—
and neither did I.

In addition to erratic mood swings and unexpected outbursts, many divorced people say they suffer from gnawing
feelings of alienation, detachment, loneliness, or *aloneness*.
Another friend describes her feelings throughout the first
six months after separation from her husband of eleven
years and father of her two children:

> I was convinced divorce was the only solution to an ever-
> worsening situation. For four years our marriage crumbled
> into a downward spiral. I tried to get Kevin to talk about
> our problems. He wouldn't talk—and going to a counselor
> together was out of the question as far as he was con-
> cerned. So I went by myself for a year—till Kevin grew so
> furious about what it cost that I decided it wasn't worth it.
> But I am thankful for that year; it helped get me back on my
> feet psychologically.
>
> My husband had only three driving interests: televi-
> sion, sex, and booze. He wasn't bad to the children; he just
> didn't do anything—he was just there. He didn't help
> with the house—no cleaning, no cooking, no lawnwork,
> no *nothing*. That pretty well describes our marriage—a lot
> of *nothing*.
>
> Strange as it seems, though, I felt an almost irresistible
> pull to go back to Kevin. I was so *alone*. Even with my having
> the kids, I felt alone. At least when I was married I could
> predict how my life was going to be. My life with Kevin,
> which had seemed so miserable, almost seemed preferable
> to the *aloneness* that engulfed me after the divorce.

After a divorce, the initial feelings of relief and the
"happily-ever-after" attitude soon fade, and a reaction much
like grief occurs, according to Esther Oshiver Fisher, author
of *Divorce: The New Freedom*. She calls divorce the death of a
marriage in which the husband and wife together with their
children are the mourners . . . the court is the cemetery
where the coffin is sealed and the dead marriage buried.

Divorce Is Bad for Your Health

Breaking up a marriage may break your health—or at least bend it badly, according to Robert L. Barker, author of *Treating Couples in Crisis.* Divorced people visit their doctors more, go to hospitals more and stay there longer, and take more time off from work because of illness. Divorced people die sooner as well. They are 30 percent more prone to cancer, 50 percent more likely to die from coronary disease, and 150 percent more likely to die in automobile accidents. Divorced men and women are also more likely to be murdered than are the married.

Other consequences of divorce can also deliver severe blows. Many men, for instance, struggle with simply "taking care of themselves," as one divorced man put it. Here is how another described his experience:

> The first three months was hell. . . . Just tracking down my apartment was a harrowing experience . . . and the housekeeping! How could I have taken for granted those chores which my wife had performed all these years, and which I now had to struggle with?
>
> After work I would find myself roaming up and down supermarket aisles, so self-conscious about being a man on what I had always considered woman's turf. . . . The dirty [clothes were] constantly out of control . . . my cooking was lousy . . . the results were stomach-turning.
>
> Insignificant details? Confessions of a male chauvinist pig? Perhaps, but at the time I saw every domestic chore as an accusation, a personal assault on my male identity. The place was a shambles. . . . How I longed for someone to take care of me![4]

Most women, in contrast, can "take care" of themselves after divorce. They are more likely to bemoan the hassles of "too little money spread too thin for two households and two kids," as one divorced woman expressed it. For some divorced women, finding a job outside the home for the first time in years—and for some, the first time ever—is their most frightening challenge.

Despite hopes that the divorce would lessen stress in the family, it often actually adds to it. While the divorced marriage partners are struggling with their own feelings of betrayal and rejection, the children need more understanding and assurance than ever. The parent who has custody, emphasizes Dr. Wallerstein, is more vulnerable to stress, has decreased psychological reserves, and "more often than not suffers from chronic economic and psychological overload while the other parent often endures feelings of isolation and alienation from his or her children." As one parent put it, "I feel like I need to be two people. I feel pulled in every direction . . . when there's nothing left to pull."

A "New Beginning" for the Children?

For most children, divorce is a far cry from a "new beginning" in the positive sense. What divorce often begins for children is a life of being torn between two divorced parents, and a life of adjusting to myriad changes, often to a new set of "steps"—a new stepparent, stepbrothers and stepsisters, and stepgrandparents.

Is divorce always bad on children? This is one of life's most difficult questions. The answer depends on each situation—how bad the marriage is, how much the children are caught up in its negative aspects, what changes in the children's lives are required by the divorce, and how the children feel about these changes. The list goes on and on.

One of the most comprehensive studies of children of divorce pooled data from eight national surveys by the National Research Center. Children of divorce compared unfavorably with other groups on eight different measures of psychological well-being, including happiness, health, and satisfaction with various aspects of life. This study also indicated that the negative effects of divorce persist throughout the lifespan much more than other research had indicated.

These research findings do not mean that divorce is bad for *all* children, of course. What it does mean is that the effects of divorce on many children may be more severe than we often think and that the effects on many children are often longer lasting than was previously believed.

No Help for the Wounded

Marriage may be difficult, but divorce can be even more difficult, partly because divorce is one of the few "passages" or significant changes couples go through in our culture for which there is no formal ritual. Birth, marriage, and death all have fairly definite formal rituals associated with them. Divorce not only has no ritual, but the divorcing partners get very little help or emotional support from others because friends and relatives simply do not know what to do. One divorced person summarized the situation by saying there is "no help for the wounded."

Christians Endure Added Problems

As if divorcing people in general did not already face seemingly insurmountable hurdles, divorcing Christians endure added problems. Some churches tend not only to be harsh on the issue of divorce but also on any church members resorting to it. Divorced people may find themselves labeled with the stigma of "sin," either tacitly or by the simple reality that the divorced individual does not "fit" anywhere. Often no classes are provided for the divorced, or if there are such classes, all too frequently a stigma is attached to them. Here is one divorced individual's account:

> After my divorce, I felt the need to "belong" somewhere more than ever. I thought my church would soothe my frayed nerves and heal my hurt. Not so! Classes were strictly for couples. Divorced people stood out like sore thumbs. I started going to another church because it had a class for singles. Sad to say, this helped very little. In fact, it was like rubbing salt in a raw wound because the class had a stigma—like a place for misfits, for failures, for the modern-day lepers who must be kept apart lest they infect all the others!

In the book *The Divorcing Christian,* Lewis R. Rambo points out that only if the spouse was blatantly, obviously "bad," does the church respond with sympathy for the "innocent" partner; but rarely are cases that clear-cut. Furthermore, church members are made to feel that "good Christians" do not have marital problems, and "good Christians" certainly never get a divorce. Many churches also teach that God can do anything, says Rambo, and that if troubled marriage partners would pray properly, God would heal the marriage, whereas Rambo, writing out of his own personal experiences, responds, "But I did pray, and God didn't save the marriage, and that makes me angry."

Then Rambo says his legalistic Christian conscience tells him that anger at God is blasphemous, so he has even more to feel guilty about. And so the burden of the divorced multiplies. Sheer weight and number of problems, some church teachings and practices, the disdainful attitude of some church friends, and the divorcing persons' own consciences add to the burden of divorced Christians.

Isn't Divorce Better Than an "Empty Shell" Marriage?

In *Divorce and the Christian: What the Bible Teaches,* Robert J. Plekker explores answers to the question, "Isn't the tragedy of a marriage without love worse than the pain of divorce?" This question is answered point-blank in *Marriage and the Family: A Christian Perspective:* "What God has joined together, let not man separate." Most people in general, including the clergy and married individuals, especially those who are *unhappily* married, admit this question-and-answer dilemma is not quite so simple; it is confusing and controversial.

Some marriage partners only *exist* under the same roof, held together by fear, guilt, economic pressures, religious convictions, apathy, or for the sake of the children. Marriages like these may be wrought with endless friction, tension, physical and emotional abuse, or misery! Or partners may keep their tensions hidden, appearing happily married to outsiders because they stay together. One family member describes this kind of marriage: "There were no ugly flare-ups—just a cold, uncaring Arctic climate devoid of any warmth."

Many partners in marriages like these ask themselves, "Isn't divorce better than an 'empty shell' marriage?" They also ask a similar thought-provoking question: "Doesn't a marriage that exists like this amount to a sham imposed by social hypocrisy?"

Two people very dear to me both found themselves in such marriages. Long before these two marriages failed, I had wondered how each tolerated their marriage partners. In both cases, however, each said as badly as they wanted out of a disappointing and wearisome relationship they never dreamt divorce would be so complicated and difficult.

Better the Second Time Around?

Hope abounds for a good marriage, even for those who have gone through the wrenching experience of divorce. Arthur Norton, family demographer for the U.S. Census Bureau, says his figures show four out of five divorced people remarry, half of them within a year of their divorces. Norton points out that second marriages in the United States, however, are more likely to end in divorce than are first marriages. "Not only that," notes Norton, "but dreams for happiness in the second marriage shatter even sooner . . . the second marriage doesn't generally last as long as the first marriage." So, divorce for many individuals fails to offer a new wonderful beginning, and for them marriage is no better the second time around.

Some Last Words

While crystallizing my thoughts for this myth, I accompanied my husband to Hawaii. He attended business meetings during the mornings and early afternoons, and I stuck to my writing schedule so we could turn into tourists the remainder of the day. Writing about divorce at first seemed ironic, if not blatantly inappropriate, while surrounded by

numerous happy honeymooners and other carefree vaca-
tioners. Yet, the surroundings actually served as a catalyst
for my writing as I wondered how many young couples just
like these happy ones in Hawaii have expressed the attitude: "If this marriage doesn't work out, I can always get a
divorce."

I wanted to stop each couple, look deep into their starry
eyes and warn them: "Shatter early in your marriage the
myth that divorce is an easy way out."

As I worked on a lanai overlooking a plush Hawaiian golf
course and sparkling beach, a curious stranger sitting
nearby asked what I was writing about. When I told her I
was writing on misconceptions about divorce, she asked me
to explain. I replied, "I am trying to get across the message
that divorce can be a positive solution to a conflict-ridden
marriage, and it should be available for those whose marriages are absolutely irreparable. But, for the majority, divorce is neither simple nor easy."

Since my audience of one seemed captivated—and silent—I continued, "I have tried simply to debunk the myth
that divorce is an easy route to a new life. I have tried to
point out some concerns and considerations that might be
helpful to those contemplating divorce, to those in the midst
of divorce, and to those who want to provide help and
encouragement to the divorced—and to those who want to
avoid going through a divorce."

At this, the stranger sat up on the edge of her chair; I
knew she wanted her turn to talk. And talk she did—at
great length and with deep emotion—about her own tortu-
ous divorce and those of several friends and relatives. She
added slowly and deliberately, "I wish I had known earlier
not only more about marriage but also more about divorce."
Then, in a voice that might well have been the echo of
thousands of other voices speaking from experience, she
said, "Divorce does not provide an easy opportunity to begin a completely new life. . . . You carry the scars of divorce with you forever."

MYTH 17:

If You Really Love Me . . .
(The Myth of Conditional Love)

"OH, 'TIS LOVE, 'tis love, that makes the world go round!" These immortal words Lewis Carroll voiced in *Alice's Adventures in Wonderland* may ring true in make-believe and fantasy, but in real-life marriage they strike a tone of unreality. When marriage partners speak the words, "If you really love me . . . ," and follow them with a certain expectation or condition, you can be sure they are dealing with a dangerous assumption—a dangerous *false* assumption! Consider these common marital myths and how they can sound the death knell to your marriage relationship.

If You Really Love Me, You Will
Never Be Attracted to Someone Else

A few years ago a popular notion predicted nearly everyone would probably have an affair sooner or later. People were saying, "Infidelity is inevitable; everyone plays around." Yet, marriage counselors estimate that no

more than one or two persons out of every ten report ever
being involved in an extramarital affair. Obviously not
everyone plays around. To argue otherwise ignores the
millions who remain faithful.

While having an affair is not inevitable, finding someone
other than your mate attractive is another matter. "It's not
uncommon to be attracted to people other than your
spouse," says New York psychiatrist Dr. Avodah K. Offit.
"Even the most monogamous men and women occasionally
have to wrestle with old-fashioned temptation."[1]

Allures and Antidotes

One appeal of affairs, say numerous individuals, is that
scintillating sensation of being found attractive—newly
in love. Victor Hugo said it well in *Les Miserables:* "The
supreme happiness of life is the conviction that we are
loved." This feeling usually "blinds people to their lover's
faults and reminds them of the days when they were
young and carefree," says Arthur Maslow, a member of the
clinical staff at New York's Ackerman Institute for Family
Therapy.

An additional allure of affairs is that, unlike marriages,
they are devoid of restrictions and obligations. And what
married person hasn't occasionally fantasized about getting away from all the demands a marriage makes on time,
effort, money, and emotions? "Lovers make few demands,"
says Maslow. "Once they start setting rules, the relationship
begins to lose its charm."[2]

To overcome these attractions, the best antidote is simply
"old-fashioned willpower," emphasizes Dr. Offit. Cutting
down on your time and association with the person you
find irresistible and finding special ways to grow closer to
your marriage partner will also help. Dr. Offit and other
marriage experts completely explode the myth voiced by
those who say, "If you really love me, you will never be
attracted to someone else." Dr. Offit concludes, "Attraction
can't be avoided. Infidelity can."[3]

Another erroneous belief is that people who are unfaithful do not love their marriage partners. While it is true that people who do not love their spouses are likely to be unfaithful, the opposite is not necessarily true. Neither is the old maxim that you cannot love two people at the same time. According to Dr. Offit, "It's quite possible to be infatuated with a lover and still care deeply about a spouse."[4]

Experts warn husbands and wives not to scoff at an unfaithful marriage partner who declares love for them. "They may in fact possess genuine love for their marriage partner," says Dr. DeFrain.[5]

A *Whack on the Side of the Head* is a book on how to break mental inertia and irrational, robotlike thinking, and to free a locked-up mind to adopt a creative outlook, opening ourselves to new possibilities and change. Attraction to another person can be that "whack on the side of the head" that makes marriage partners realize there are some changes they need to make. Perhaps the partners have marital inertia and have been taking each other for granted. Or perhaps they have relegated all their attention to their careers, to aging parents, or to a host of other matters. This "whack on the side of the head" may be the shock galvanizing a husband and wife into an open and honest sharing of their cares and concerns—and their hopes and dreams for their marriage.

Some couples need a professional counselor to help facilitate this kind of constructive communication while other couples are able to restore harmony on their own. Partners who profess to love each other are more likely to be able to rebuild their relationship on their own. If one or both partners are riddled with doubts, indifference, or bitterness, then help from a counselor usually proves invaluable.

One husband and wife who fit this description did seek the assistance of a good marriage counselor. Says the wife, "We are not embarrassed to admit we needed help. Now we encourage people whose marriages are suffering to get help. It's the smart thing to do." The husband adds, "It is money well spent."

If You Really Love Me,
You Won't Expect Me to Change

Expecting changes in our mate runs counter to a basic myth of marriage. In spite of the staggering statistics on divorce, the "get-married-and-live-happily-ever-after" myth is as strong as ever. I distinctly remember the admonition of a speaker Del and I heard early in our marriage: "Acceptance is the key to a happy marriage. Let each other be who you are." The speaker went on to comment on how both husbands and wives come preassembled with no instructions about how to correct major flaws in the manufacturing and each wants to "correct" everything about the other according to some preconceived notion of the "perfect" spouse. The best approach, according to this speaker, is to accept your spouse "as is" and not to expect changes.

While it may be unrealistic as well as unfair to expect basic personality or character changes in your mate, it is reasonable and realistic to expect some changes in your mate and in yourself as you travel along the marital journey. The joining together of two separate lives into a smoothly running, satisfying relationship takes some changes, some compromises, and some sacrifices—not dreadful soul-searing ones, but at least a minimal level of each. Some of one's legitimate desires and some of one's ways of doing things simply must be given up or modified for the sake of the marriage.

Growth Requires Change—Even in Marriage

A growing, fulfilling marriage requires some emotional, financial, and sexual changes, and more self-discipline than needed in the single life. Self-discipline in my marriage has been particularly difficult in the area of bossiness.

Del and I were in our mid-twenties and relatively well set in our ways when we married. For example, we both had our own way of handling the checkbook. And Del's way was nowhere similar to my way. Since he had undergraduate and graduate degrees in accounting, as well as the letters

C.P.A. after his name, I threw in the towel on our different opinions about checkbooks. I have conceded that he is the expert. I try very earnestly to be accommodating because a neat, organized, and balanced checkbook means so much to Del. (But I still think he is awfully picky to insist on recording every check, writing all numbers legibly, and reconciling the checkbook every month to the exact penny!)

Del and I have other areas and issues where we have had to squelch our innate urges to be bossy. Once when I was doing something (I do not remember what now) but Del recalled I had threatened to kill if he tried to tell me how to do it. So he carefully avoided offering advice. Instead, he said as impersonally as he could: "The most difficult thing in the world is to know how to do something *right* and to watch somebody else do it *wrong*, without comment."

Not only do couples have to make some changes in ways they relate to each other, they must also deal with cultural changes brought on in recent years. The altering of male and female roles, for example, and the shifting of modern responsibilities have tested the tensile strength of many marriages.

Individuals who want a fulfilling marriage should never fear or even avoid changing habits, attitudes, reactions, and responses. They should never hide behind the adage, "You can't teach an old dog new tricks," because it simply is not true. We all have within us an amazing ability to change, to adapt. We all have hidden strengths and remarkable capacities for growth and creative change. One individual whose marriage was about to the breaking point said, "I finally concluded that it would be better to bend than to break. I also have found out to my amazement that if I take one step toward making some changes my wife wanted, she takes two steps toward changes I wanted." The wife added, "I just wish we had started earlier in our marriage telling each other honestly but kindly how we really felt about certain things and then bargaining, saying, 'If I do this . . . , will you do that . . . ?'"

A marriage either grows or deteriorates; it never stays the same. It is sort of like an airplane in flight. It must stay in motion. It cannot simply stay still and be suspended in space at the same time, or it will fall crashing to the ground.

Each year more than 150,000 American couples stay in flight, so to speak, and mark their golden wedding anniversaries, according to an article called "What Makes a Marriage as Good as Gold?"[6] In this article Dr. James Peterson, a marital therapist and expert on aging at the University of Southern California, emphasized, "But the fact that a couple has stayed together fifty years doesn't necessarily prove they have a happy marriage." According to Peterson, some long-married couples can be classified as "survivors" who have stayed together for a variety of reasons—children, religion, apathy—and have little open conflict but also little satisfaction. There are, however, long-term marriages that are still happy and rewarding. The reason, according to Dr. Peterson and other experts, is because the partners are flexible enough to change, and they continue through the years to change, to adapt, to modify, to compromise, to attune, to grow.

Couples whose marriages have not survived often blame the split on changes in both partners after marriage. I think in most cases that is exactly opposite of the real reason. I think it is because one or both *refused* to change. They retained their old habits, cherished their old prejudices, preserved their old values, honored their own selfishness, held tenaciously to their own private purposes and agenda, and clung to the fanciful notion that "If you really love your marriage partner, you will never expect him (or her) to change."

If You Really Love Me, You'll Always Trust Me

The story is told of a man who left his house every night, telling his wife he was going hunting. He returned home every night about the same time, several hours after his wife had fallen asleep. Some weeks after this routine began, the wife went out to the barn one evening after her husband had supposedly gone hunting—and found his gun still there.

For several days the wife's mind ran wild; she could hardly bear to imagine what her husband might be doing during those evening hours. For almost a week she studied every word he said, every movement, every facial expression. *He seems so devoted,* she thought. *How could he possibly be doing this to me?*

Without a word, she planned her revenge. As he returned home late one evening and walked ever so carefully into the bedroom so not to awaken his wife, she stood behind the door, his gun in her hands. When her husband turned to sit down on the bed, she lifted the gun, took aim, and pulled the trigger. He never knew what hit him.

The next morning one of the first people to see the wife was a neighbor and foreman of a lumber mill several miles away. When the wife told him why she had shot her husband, the man's face froze in disbelief. "Your husband," he spoke slowly and deliberately, "was working every night at the lumber mill so he could surprise you by buying you a better house."

Not all real-life situations turn out as dramatic as this fictionalized one, of course; but suspicion and mistrust in many relationships are equally as destructive. And stories like this reinforce the myth that if you really love your marriage partner, you will enjoy complete trust.

On the other hand, complete, absolute trust can also destroy a relationship—not in a sensational way, but destroy it nevertheless. When there is blind trust, taking your partner for granted is almost certain, and one partner taking the other for granted, or both taking each other for granted, is almost always destructive.

However, if you consider your mate quite capable of attracting members of the opposite sex, and likely to respond to this attention if neglected or mistreated within the marriage, you will probably increase your own displays of attention, caring, and affection. One psychologist who has studied this topic extensively has this to say about it:

A "tinge of insecurity" keeps a marriage viable, meaningful, even exciting. It prevents one from taking things for granted, growing fat or sloppy, paying more attention to the job than necessary, or displaying disrespect. What is more, it fosters and maintains the level of love and affectionate caring that makes marriage worth preserving."[7]

If You Really Love Me, You'll Work Hard at Making Our Marriage a Really Good One

As is true for most myths, there is a small grain of truth in this one, but that small grain has become magnified as being the whole, unadulterated truth. First of all, it's always dangerous to place conditions on love. And second, all marriages, regardless of how much the two partners love each other, require teamwork, compromise, self-discipline, restraint, and mutual respect—all of which demand some effort, or work, at times.

If you love your marriage partner, you probably will be motivated to work hard at making the marriage a good one. But here is the glitch: Working hard in itself does not guarantee a good marriage. This fact of life does not, of course, indicate that couples should *not* work at having an amicable relationship. But it is a myth to expect marital bliss if one simply "works hard" at having a successful marriage. Diane S. Richmond and David E. Garland, the co-authors of *Beyond Companionship—Christians in Marriage*, agree: "We can work as hard as we like at our marriage, but labor alone will not ensure success."

The marriage of one of my relatives fell prey to this "work hard" myth. She was doing all that she knew how to salvage her relationship and maker her marriage work out. Difficulties mounted and she felt the strain in her emotional muscle as she struggled to "Hang in there!" as many well-meaning friends and relatives kept advising her. The problem was, she was already doing that and it wasn't helping. For years she had been told in so many words, "Keep working and your marriage will work out." These words were like salt in a raw wound. They remind me of the situation described in James 2:16 where a cold, hungry person is told to "stay warm and eat hearty" (TLB). Instead of helping, these kinds of words add to the victim's frustrations, hopelessness, and sense of guilt and failure.

Like my relative, most of us go into marriage with high expectations and enthusiasm to do whatever it takes to "Live happily ever after." However, many simply do not have the knowledge and skills that marriage demands. Or they may have emotional hangups that prevent them from creating a mutually satisfying marriage. For instance, from early childhood on, each of us develops idealized models in our minds for our marriage—husband, wife, father, mother, and all the other family roles. And few humans can live up to these idealized images, no matter how hard we work. What most of us need is not "more work" but increased understanding of ourselves and others and more realistic expectations of ourselves and our marriage.

Another loophole in this myth is the assumption that marriage is the sole result of whatever actions and attitudes the two partners bring to the marriage. This viewpoint sees marriage as a closed system responding only to what the two mates do or do not do. Many forces and influences outside the marriage affect the quality of the marriage itself—for example, the extended families, in-laws, friends, neighborhood, employment, income, health, illness, or death, and even such factors as natural events and disasters and the physical space and privacy of the home.[8]

One outside force which has had untold effect on marriages has been the church's attitude toward it. At times I have called it the Christian conspiracy, or the immaculate deception. Everyone assumes that every other couple lives up to the perfect marriage in which both partners always love each other and live in perfect God-inspired harmony. Hardly anyone will ever admit to having problems or doubts. If they do, the church's advice most likely will be: "Pray about it and everything will work out."

Don't get me wrong. I believe in the power of prayer, and I know from my own experience that Tennyson's observation is true: "More things are wrought by prayer than this world dreams of." But most of us mortal married souls need

some practical, down-to-earth instructions for working on
our marriage to go along with the spiritual guideposts.

When churches sponsor marriage enrichment activities,
the announcement is made that they are for healthy couples, not ones needing therapy. The intent of this announcement is, I suppose, to remove any stigma of attending the
activity. But it also sends the message that to be experiencing trouble in your marriage is bad; so couples do not admit
to having difficulty and continue the lonely downward spiral all alone, thinking everybody else's marriage is okay. Or
they continue to fake it. They work hard at maintaining
the image of a happily married couple. They sign up for the
marriage enrichment activities, put on their false smiley-
face masks, attend the activities, and go through the too-
often trivial exercises like pious little marriage machines.
They continue the acceptable religious deception while the
mortar holding their marriage together quietly crumbles.

When work turns to hard labor, when compromise turns
to coercion, when teamwork turns to tedium, when unity
turns to utility, then the cruel truth of this myth is seen.
Then we can understand more clearly that marriage is more
than the sum of the parts. Without love, as well as adequate
people skills and the ability to break through the facades
and deal with the realities of the relationship, all the *work* in
the world will not keep holy wedlock from turning into
unholy deadlock.

*   *   *   *

"If you really love me, . . ." These words can be lethal to
a promising relationship. Do not expect more of love than it
is humanly possible to deliver. In a speech I heard long ago,
the speaker quoted Rabbi Julius Gordon offering some insightful words on this matter:

> Love is not blind —it sees more, not less. But because
> it sees more, it is willing to see less.

MYTH 18:

Anger Has No Place in Marriage

PANDORA WAS THE world's first woman, according to Greek mythology. She was given a box, so the story goes, which, if opened, would release its contents—all the world's ills. Curiosity got the best of Pandora, so she opened the box and sure enough, its contents escaped. Some say anger was among the awful contents of Pandora's box and that anger remains the world's worst emotion to be avoided in marriage at all costs.

Not so! Just as this story about Pandora belongs in the realm of make-believe, so does this myth. Anger in and of itself is not bad, "wrong," or sinful. Anger works like a smoke detector. It warns us of danger so we can take appropriate actions. It is a friend in disguise, identifying the areas in which we need to make adjustments in our marital relationship.

Recognizing anger for what it is and handling it constructively prevents us from wearing false masks, playing marital charades, and carrying out our marital roles day in and day out in a dreary daze of deception. Honest feelings, expressed with sensitivity and kindness, forestall seething resentment and hostility and help vitalize the trusting, dynamic relationship we all long for. One husband put it plainly: "Anger helps us pinpoint problem spots in the marriage so we can do something about them."

Marriage counselor and professor of sociology at the University of California Dr. Carlfred Broderick observes: "I see scores of marriages in which the partners bottle up their anger. They may think they have a 'good' marriage. They may never say a cross word to each other. But neither do they have any warmth or sparkle in their relationship."[1] These often are the marriages in which one or both partners operate under the deadening slogan, "Peace at any price."

Some couples, to avoid anger, take on an air of indifference. But George Bernard Shaw believed such indifference is actually more cruel than anger. "The worse sin towards our fellow creatures is not to hate them, but to be indifferent to them: that's the essence of inhumanity," he wrote. My husband once spoke volumes when, infuriated at me over some long-forgotten marital infraction, he declared, "I love you too much *not* to be angry!"

I Have Reason Enough to Be Angry

Individuals possess different personalities, come from different family backgrounds, hold different expectations, are born with different metabolic rates, develop different needs, and often even operate out of different sides of the brain. Is it any wonder, then, that wedlock can turn into hammerlock? Voicing a feeling that we all have had at one time or another, one distraught husband declared, "I have reason enough to be angry!"

While it is true that a great deal of conflict can be destructive to a relationship and that mismanaged anger can strike the final death blow, it is unrealistic to think that two mortals can live side by side without occasional clashes. This rigid pattern tends to create a great gap in trust and unity, as the authors of *The Mirages of Marriage* point out:

> How can spouses trust each other if they never have any disagreements? How does each know what the other really thinks or feels if he is accommodating . . . all the time? For all anyone can tell one spouse may secretly hate the other's guts.[2]

Paul and Beth both secretly harbored anger toward each other. Beth resented Paul working evenings and leaving her alone to cope with the growing-up problems of their teenage son, Bill, and their eight-year-old daughter, Amy.

For months, feeling that Paul was shirking his parental duties, Beth stifled her anger—until late one night, she finally exploded. "After clearing the air," Beth recalls, "Paul and I made some startling discoveries about each other. What I thought was indifference on Paul's part turned out to be silent hostility toward me. He thought I wanted to take over our children's lives. He felt left out and hurt—and angry."

Paul says he had come to feel like nothing more than a robot breadwinner. "I wanted to be an understanding father and a loving husband," he stresses. "And I was bitter at Beth for robbing me of those opportunities; meanwhile, she was angry with me for ducking my responsibilities with the children. This was an important lesson for both of us. When we feel that we have a reason to be angry, we share it with each other, knowing that being angry doesn't mean we don't love each other. We enjoy a lot more mutual respect now."

Beth shares some additional insight on this idea of love and anger: "No one can get angrier than children do at their parents, and parents can get really incensed with their children. Yet we rarely question the fact of love between parent and child. We often fail to recognize that it works the same way between marriage partners." If we fail to understand how people who love each other "have reason enough to be angry," we may jump to the conclusion that love is dead and bury it prematurely.

I Never Get Angry . . . I'm Depressed Most of the Time

The Wall Street Journal contends that an epidemic of depression is sweeping our nation, and many experts say that more humans suffer from depression than from any other malady. To add to this plight, not many people even understand what causes depression. And certainly very few of them think that anger is related to depression since these two emotions seem so opposite from each other. One woman's comment reflects the colossal misunderstanding many people have about how anger and depression are interrelated: "I never get angry . . . I'm depressed most of the time."

Not everyone agrees about all the causes of depression; but two of the causes, most agree, are related to how people handle anger. First of all, most people grow up not having good role models, so they never learn to handle anger constructively. The reason our Creator gave us the capacity to feel anger is to prepare us and alert us to handle threats in our environment. Threats no longer exist in the form of wild animals and malicious enemy tribes, but they exist in the form of psychological threats of hurt, frustration, fear, and wounded pride. When we handle these threats ineffectively, we experience a sense of helplessness and inadequacy and become depressed.

The second cause of depression is similar: When we conclude we are failures at handling external problems, we may turn our anger inward on ourselves, concentrating on our failures, chastising ourselves for even the smallest mistakes, zapping ourselves with bitter putdowns, stripping ourselves of self-respect, making ourselves feel less and less significant, and reducing our feelings of self-worth to pitifully dangerous levels. And sometimes we have help from others who want to cut us down. It is helpful to remember Eleanor Roosevelt's advice: "No one can make you feel inferior without your consent." When people realize this important truth, they have put firmly into place the cornerstone for resisting depression brought on by anger turned inward.

When we express anger appropriately, we "let off steam" before our psyches explode and cave in on themselves in a bottomless pool of depression. Anger rightly channeled can be as good for marriages as it is for individuals.

How to Think Straight When You Cannot See Straight

Now that I've outlined some of the benefits of appropriately handled anger, you may be thinking, *OK, so it can be beneficial. But just how do I go about doing that? How can I think straight when I'm so mad I can't see straight?* Here are some useful guidelines for dealing constructively with anger in the marriage relationship. To begin with, partners must discard the misconception that anger is a sin. The Bible never said anger is a sin; that viewpoint is man's faulty interpretation and a gross oversimplification. One of the most oft-quoted scriptures says, "Be angry but do not sin; do not let the sun go down on your anger" (Eph. 4:26, RSV). This scripture does not say not to be angry; it says not to sin. The point is that it is okay to be angry, but you must be careful not to sin in the way you express your anger.

An essential for carrying out this mandate is found in another scripture: "Stop lying to each other; tell the truth, for we are parts of each other and when we lie to each other we are hurting ourselves" (Eph. 4:25, TLB). So, begin by recognizing anger as a normal emotion and avoid denying its existence.

Second, make a commitment to each other to be open and honest about your feelings. When you make it a habit to avoid facades, deception, and disavowing your anger, you create new opportunities for both of you to be genuine and to be your real and true selves. When you strip your relationship of the myth that anger has no place in marriage, you can build a relationship of trust, sharing, and mutual support and encouragement—a surer foundation for a vital and satisfying marriage.

Warning: Handling your anger honestly and openly does not mean "letting it all hang out." Counting to ten before you blow up is age-old advice that is as good as ever. Here is a scripture spelling it out: "He that is slow to anger is better than the mighty; and he that ruleth his spirit than he that taketh a city" (Prov. 16:32, KJV). This scripture emphasizes yet another universal truth: "A soft answer turns away wrath, but a harsh word stirs up anger" (Prov. 15:1, RSV).

Applying these scriptures to the ups and downs of marriage does not come naturally or easily. But marriage partners can *learn* to apply them. In fact, all of our emotional responses are learned. Anger is no exception. My grandmother knew this, and I remember her telling Del and me early in our marriage that an important key to keeping our marital boat afloat and on an even keel was simply this: "Learn not to get angry both at the same time."

Also avoid dumping all your gripes and grievances out on the table and then doing nothing about them. You may think you feel better for "getting things off your chest," but over the long run this "garbage dumping" hurts a marriage more than it helps. If something is serious enough to be bothering you, it deserves agreeing upon a time when both of you are willing to give it your full attention. Work together on a plan of action. Then set definite times throughout the next week or so to check in with each other and evaluate how well your plan is working. If necessary, modify your plan to make it reasonable and realistic.

For most couples the best plans require both partners to modify their behavior. The negotiated agreements need to be things you both care about and are red flags in your relationship. For example, one husband made this offer to his wife: "I will not say anything derogatory about your relatives if you will quit leaving your dirty ashtray in the family room."

Another important skill to learn which often dissipates anger or prevents it from building up is the willingness to admit you made a mistake and to sincerely say, "I'm sorry." The popular movie, *Love Story,* misled lovers the world over into thinking "Love is never having to say you're sorry."

That was okay for those two Hollywood lovers; it made for a dramatic episode in the movie. But who really wants to be married to someone who'll never utter an apology? Judith Viorst, a popular journalist, responded to this issue by saying, "Love means never having to say you're sorry. Except when it's your fault. Or when it's his fault but he's too immature to admit it. Or when it's nobody's fault but someone is looking for a scapegoat. Or when you haven't spoken all evening and someone needs to break the ice. . . ."

You may handle your anger constructively, but your mate may have a problem. The authors of *Aggress-Less: How to Turn Anger and Aggression into Positive Action* outline some basic steps for calming an angry person:

1. *Be an example of calmness yourself.* Remember your overall goal is to solve the problem, not to defeat or conquer the other person. Model calmness through your words, facial expression, posture and gestures, what you say, and your tone of voice.

2. *Encourage talking.* Show your mate you want to understand better by asking open-ended questions beginning with *what, why,* or *how.* Ask only one question at a time, and be as specific as possible. Respond by attentive listening.

3. *Show by your attitude, attentive listening, and your comments that you appreciate the other person's openness and willingness to talk.* A response like this, for example, may help: "I really appreciate your telling me how you feel. I did not know that made you angry . . . I will try not to do it anymore."

4. *Avoid interrupting.* Pay close attention, facing the other person squarely. With sensitivity, try to "read between the lines" to fully understand what the other person is trying to tell you.

5. *Show understanding.* Concentrate more on what your mate is feeling than on what words are being said. Called empathy, this skill is essential to calming an angry person. It requires your putting yourself in the other person's place. It cannot be faked; it must be genuine.

6. *Reassure your mate.* Direct your reassuring efforts and comments at reducing threats, clearing up misunderstandings, and doing your part to work out the problem

calmly. A comment like this may be helpful: "I'm really interested in working this out with you."

7. *Help save face.* Do whatever it takes to increase your mate's willingness to join you in trying to defeat the problem, not you. Make it easy for your mate to back off or retreat gracefully. Don't humiliate your mate in front of others. Avoid comments that are provoking, belittling, critical, threatening, or impatient. Remember that the marriage relationship and the dignity of each partner are more important than proving one partner is "right" and another is "wrong."[3]

Words from Aristotle capture the essence of handling anger constructively in marriage: "A person who is praised is the one who is angry for the right reasons, with the right people, and also in the right way and at the right time for the right length of time."

So, finally back to Pandora, who let all human ills—especially anger—escape when she opened the box. Throughout the ages since that make-believe story was first told, anger has received an undeserved rap. Clearly, it is an injurious myth that anger has no place in marriage. Indifference, apathy, not caring enough even to get angry—these, and not anger, are the forewarnings of a marriage in trouble. When couples care enough to express anger appropriately, then marital growth and satisfaction are enhanced. And hope survives, even as it did when Pandora's box was opened.

MYTH 19:

Spouses Argue Most over Money (and Sex)

FOR DECADES PEOPLE have pointed their accusing fingers at money and sex as the two hottest topics generating matrimonial misery. Writer James E. Kilgore describes the age-old artillery of marital warfare:

> In the "good old days" the two basic weapons were money and sex. The husband usually controlled the finances. If the wife was "a good girl," she got some money. If not, she didn't. She usually controlled the sex. If he was a "good boy," he got some; if not, he waited.[1]

Today, even more than in the "good old days," money seems to be used as a weapon. But after twenty-five years of irrationally debating differences of opinions about money with my husband, I have concluded it is a blatant myth that when mates are haggling over money it is really money they are talking about. Money is simply the tangible weapon they have chosen to wage their war over underlying psychological issues such as power control, independence, and self-image.

Only when couples recognize the core cause, the basic underlying issue of their "money arguments," will they be in a position to work out a mutually satisfying resolution to their conflict. Only when two partners sort out fiction from fact—separate their thoughts about dollars and cents versus their beliefs about what money represents psychologically to each of them—can they dismount their roller-coaster ride and quit falsely accusing that innocuous paper called money as the chief engineer driving them on their collision course.

Astute readers may realize that the topic of sex somehow is being left behind in this discussion. With a sense of humor, some may quip, "So, what's new? Sex often gets put on the back burner." The issue of money in marriage and what it really means is complicated enough, but that of sex is even more symbolic and emotionally explosive. I plan to give that mystery some serious and undivided study the next twenty-five years of my marriage—my husband has generously offered to assist me. In the meantime, let's concentrate our attention on the myth that when couples are haggling over money, it is actually money that is the problem. I think you will agree some of the generalizations I offer about money also apply to sex.

Money Bestows Power

Money is inextricably bound up with attitudes of power and independence! Having money allows a certain freedom and bestows power. Lack of money (or lack of perceived or real freedom to use it) preempts power and confers dependence. More than any of us romantic souls ever wish to admit, money is the power base of relationships. Money on one level seems to be the antithesis of the love we say is the underlying reason for marriage. On another level, however, money is essential for love to flourish.

In a book called *Making Peace with Your Partner*, H. Norman Wright includes an insightful chapter called "Give Me Power." From that chapter here is a commentary in a nutshell on the myth that when couples haggle over money, money is the real issue:

> Power! Control! More power! More control! Nations want power, corporations strive for power, politicians want power, interest groups want power. It seems that everyone has this determined drive to gain more power and control. Marriages are not immune from this unquenchable thirst. In fact, power struggles are one of the biggest perpetrators of conflict in marriages. We hear about specific issues that couples argue about but underlying many of them is a power struggle.[2]

Trends Complicating the Meaning of Money

Society's increasing complexity is adding fuel to the fire of how partners relate to one another in marital and money matters. Two trends especially complicate the issue of what money really means to marriage partners and how they use it as a weapon or as leverage in their day-to-day negotiations:

- More and more women joining the work force outside the home

- Rampant materialism—that is, an absorbing concern with buying a better house, more furnishings, a newer car, nicer clothes.

These trends provide subtle—and sometimes not so subtle—pressure on couples. Let's look at some ways pressure is felt as one partner tries to exert power or control over the other, using money as a weapon.

Women working outside the home. When the wife enters or returns to the work force outside the home, couples find a new set of issues facing them. In a chapter called "Money and Power," the author of *A Loving Conspiracy* speaks to this point:

Undoubtedly, when women start to earn money after occu-
pying a more dependent position, that alters the power
structure in the marriage. No other factor can create such a
difference in the marital relationship, nor cause such
strains, equal to those of having children, on it. Becoming a
working woman has repercussions far beyond the job itself.[3]

Traditionally, the man brought home the bacon, and he
made the decisions about it after he brought it home. If the
wife made any decisions about it, she did so only because
the husband had granted her that authority. But when the
wife helps bring home the bacon, she may think she has the
right to help decide *who* cooks, *how* to cook it, and *when* to
cook it. Consider the case of Danielle and Kent, as described by Danielle:

> Kent always thought he was the boss of our home and that
> he could decide, without my questioning, how we should
> spend our money. He decided when we needed a new car,
> when we needed a better apartment or house, when we
> should spend extra money on clothes, when we could take
> a vacation. Not only that, he thought it was his right to
> choose *what* to buy. I got tired of him treating me like I
> didn't have any feelings or good sense. Of course, he usu-
> ally made very good decisions. But money was not the
> point. I just wanted input on decisions that affected me.
> After the children started to school and I went back to
> work, I had more courage to make myself heard. After all, I
> worked and put money in the bank account, too.

When Kent and Danielle met with a marriage counselor,
Kent's fears about his masculinity came out. He felt that to
be the head of the house, he had to be "strong." He believed
it would reflect weakness on his role if he allowed any
"feminine foolishness" (his words), like choosing a car
partly because of color, to enter into any financial decision
making. So money per se was not the issue in their strife;
Kent was simply using money as the weapon in his desperate struggle for power and a feeling of male supremacy or
self-worth. He finally recognized what he was actually

doing and that he was fighting a losing battle because *demanding* power or supremacy does not work in marriages. In fact, it usually jeopardizes the goodwill essential for a happy marriage.

The situation of Harold and Nell was quite different. Nell had worked her way up in a prosperous advertising agency while Harold had enjoyed a few minor promotions with little pay increases. When Nell was offered a plum of a position in the agency's headquarters 200 miles away, Harold listed all the expenses the move would require. He had convinced himself and tried to convince Nell that her promotion was "not worth it in dollars and cents." What was most at stake, of course, was not the dollars and cents but Harold's pride. Nell's taking this promotion would highlight his rather lackluster job, and moving to another city because of his wife's promotion was more than his male ego could handle.

As more women enter the work force, this situation is developing more frequently in marriages. Only when couples recognize that the money per se is usually not the critical issue can they handle this non-traditional dilemma in a constructive way.

Rampant materialism. The overemphasis in today's society on the accumulation of material possessions puts a heavy burden on many married couples and is frequently the real core of their conflicts over money. Materialism is the belief that *things* bring happiness, and the more things you have the more "successful" and important you are. Materialism pushes couples to buy bigger and better homes, more expensive cars, and fancier clothes (designer labels, of course!). All of these visible, tangible things are the yardstick by which the worth of the individual owner is measured. Materialism, unchecked and unbridled, can choke a good marriage to death.

Rex, for example, earns enough to provide for his family very well, but he goes overboard and buys extravagant gifts for his wife, Angie, and their teen-age daughter. Angie has told Rex over and over again that she wishes he would spend less time working and making money and more time with her and their daughter. "We don't need the expensive things he buys us," says Angie. "And our daughter is getting the wrong idea that *things* are all that matter." Rex simply finds it easier to buy things than to spend time with his family; money and the things it will buy are Rex's substitute for the affection he is unable to express in more meaningful and lasting ways.

Materialism seldom satisfies the deep emotional needs human beings have, even though people caught up in it often think "more money" would solve all their problems and make them happy. The scripture, "For the love of money is the root of all evil" (1 Tim. 6:10, KJV) is more likely to be seriously believed and practiced the way an acquaintance of mine jokingly expressed it: "The root of all evil is the *lack* of money."

The Real Sources of Conflict

Four different sources of conflict seem to cause many of the arguments couples superficially blame on money. Social conditioning, personality, circumstances, and lack of understanding about financial management are often the real culprits. Let's examine how they—and not money per se—create conflict in marriage.

Social conditioning. The attitudes of parents toward money profoundly influence the attitudes their children carry into their own marriages. Children reared in a family where "conspicuous consumption" is of primary importance, for example, will usually form their attitudes and judge their own life and success by these attitudes. People reared in homes where thrift is a virtue generally are thrifty as adults. People reared with the middle-class values of postponing present satisfaction to ensure future rewards will generally live out this value in their own family.

Some persons, of course, may renounce the values they were exposed to as children. But most of the time they simply live out these same values and attitudes in their adult life. Whatever choices individuals make as adults, they are influenced by the social or family conditioning of their childhood.

Stories of my grandmother's financial struggles after her husband died, leaving her with three young daughters to fend for, made a frightening and indelible impression on me as a young girl. And the untimely death of my own father before I was old enough to remember him also forged a strong influence on my thinking about money. My grandmother owned and managed a restaurant during my growing-up years; I saw numerous women who had minimal skills eking out an existence. I knew from firsthand experience the challenge of rearing a family on a limited income. All these experiences conditioned my attitudes. I was determined to be financially independent when I grew up. My husband has always recognized and respected my deep-seated need to work outside the home and knows that I could survive financially if something happened to him— as it did to my father and my grandfather. In our case, being a two-career family has strengthened our marriage. We stay together because we want to, not because financial constraints force us to.

All individuals bring to their marriages attitudes influenced by their early social development, and it is important to recognize them for what they are. Ruth Stafford Peale once explained how she and her husband Norman Vincent Peale brought to their marriage different ideas about money. Evidently Dr. Peale's family had suffered through some fairly grim economic times during his growing up. Mrs. Peale said that in the early years of their marriage he would become overly concerned about providing for their children, for his early social conditioning had stuck with him, as it does with all of us. Note how she handled the situation:

> At one time, I would have argued with him, would have brought out the books and shown him how I had planned for those necessary purchases. But by then, I knew that his reaction was not really to the current situation at all. It

was to voices a small boy had heard long ago: "How will we pay the grocer's bill?" And I'd learned better than to fight phantoms.[4]

Personality. People may say that they are arguing about money, but the actual, underlying issue may be the extreme differences in certain personality traits. In spite of the clashes created, sometimes it may be fortunate that mates are opposite on some traits.

For example, if one mate is exceedingly unrealistic and irresponsible when it comes to money, then it is undoubtedly a stroke of good fortune if the other mate is somewhat opposite. Even though the two partners may butt heads a lot, the more responsible one may save them from financial ruin. In this case, as in many others when personality traits are diverse, marriage partners need to recognize that the crux of their conflict is the differences in their personalities more than the money per se. When they see clearly the actual issues that are creating their conflict, then they can more constructively work out a balanced truce—and, perhaps, keep the checkbook balanced too!

Circumstances. Money problems are not always caused by inadequate income or unusual financial needs. Some marriage counselors estimate, in fact, that only one couple out of every ten experiencing money problems attributes their problems to *inadequate* income.

Whatever the problems and the basic, underlying cause, particular circumstances can sometimes trigger financial impasses. Some of these circumstances can be predicted reasonably well, while others are not so predictable. Because of the media-fed appetite for more and better things, many couples simply spend more money than they make. An unexpected illness, expensive car repairs, or the loss of a job or myriad other emergencies can roughen the waters of an otherwise smooth-sailing marriage. Kate explains how unexpected circumstances destroyed her marriage to Jack:

It seemed like from the very start of our marriage things had a way of going wrong. During the first year of our marriage, Jack had a wreck. It wasn't his fault, but it cost us a lot of money anyway. Insurance didn't cover all the car repairs or his doctor bills.

Then I had to quit working when I got pregnant; I was so sick the first three months I didn't feel like doing anything, much less getting out to a job. Then we decided to go ahead and have our second baby so they could grow up together. But both children had allergies—and a lot of doctor bills that kept our budget drained.

I had thought I'd go back to work at least part-time when the girls started school, but my first job didn't last long. I was a nervous wreck from the job and never in a very good frame of mind to be a loving mother when I got home each day. And, then, I also wanted to be able to attend their parties and to help out with things at school.

I always felt guilty that I had let Jack down since I had told him I'd go back to work after a while. But then I was angry at him because he thought the girls were 100 percent my responsibility even when I was working. We argued so much, the job just wasn't worth it all.

We were getting back on our feet when someone stole Jack's tools. Boy, things were explosive around the house for a while. Jack felt like it was someone in his work crew . . . that really hurt. But I told him he didn't have to take all $1,000 out on us at home.

The next bad thing at work was they told Jack they were going to have to either let some of the men go or they could take a pay cut. Things were so bad in the economy, Jack felt a partial job was better than no job at all, so he took a pay cut.

I tried to tell Jack back before we married he should've taken his dad up on his offer to send him to school. But he wouldn't listen, and he really blows a fuse if I say anything about it.

Then Jack's mother got sick. We didn't have to help with bills, but Jack felt like he needed to go see her often—and that took money. And Jack's brother wanted to go but couldn't afford the trip, so Jack loaned him money. Then his brother was laid off his job; he never did pay Jack back.

All these different circumstances just seemed to wear us down. Sure, other couples had worse things happen to them, and they made it. It just seemed like it was more than *we* could handle. I used to sit and cry and think, *I wish I could run away and hide from all these problems.* And that's exactly what Jack did. He just left. Looking back, I wish we could've pulled together more rather than letting everything that happened to us pull us apart.

Fortunately, most couples are not plagued with so many unforeseen and debilitating circumstances as Jack and Kate, but every married couple goes through some predictable circumstances or phases that affect their finances and marital serenity. The honeymoon stage usually finds both working, so they are relatively well off. Couples who manage to save some of their money during this stage take some of the pressure off in the next stage, the having-babies period.

When the first child is born, expenses skyrocket, often more than even the most prepared couples anticipate. The wife generally stops work, at least for a while, so income goes down while needs go up. Often a second child is born, increasing the financial pinch. Most couples say this is a difficult period to manage well the money, time, and energy and to keep the marriage on an even keel. Unexpected circumstances, like illnesses, or ones for which there is no financial provision, can throw a marriage into an emotional tailspin.

It is also during the stage of marriage when the wife is home with the young children, trying to make ends meet, that she feels emotionally trapped. Circumstances do usually improve, however, when the children are in school. Sometimes the wife/mother returns to work outside the home strengthening their financial situation. Then, when children start attending college, the financial strain may reappear, especially if circumstances have not allowed for the accumulation of a college fund.

Circumstances enveloping the couple after the children have left home and during their retirement may be exceedingly positive, negative, or simply a vacuum. So much depends on circumstances all along the way to that point and how the couple has handled whatever circumstances happened to fall their lot. Couples may say they argue about money, but in many instances the particular circumstances actually create the problems. In the absence of certain circumstances, there would undoubtedly be less conflict over money.

Understanding of money management. Another source of conflict is the understanding—or lack of understanding—of money management that two partners bring to the marriage scene. Unfortunately, even college-educated individuals, often bring a paucity of financial know-how to marriage. Many simply do not comprehend the basic rule of economics: You cannot spend more than you make; over time there always comes a day of reckoning. The second essential rule they fail to comprehend is that conflict is often not a question of dollars and cents but of attitudes and emotions. I was reminded forcefully of this truth recently after leaving the gift shop at Pearl Harbor at the USS Arizona Memorial. Let me explain.

Several years ago when we moved, we discovered just how many hundreds of pounds of books we had accumulated—our books cost as much to move as did all the rest of our household possessions. We made a firm pact at that time never to buy another book until we conferred with each other—a sort of "cooling off" period so the emotion of the moment would not sweep us off our feet. Then, on our business-leisure trip to Hawaii, Del found me in front of a marvelous display in a small shop, savoring the taste of an exotic blend of coffee. "You are not going to buy that eight-dollar bag of coffee, are you?" he one-tenth asked, nine-tenths commanded. Pouting and feeling slighted, I left the shop without purchasing the coffee and caught the bus to Pearl Harbor.

After the tour of the USS Arizona Memorial at Pearl Harbor, we browsed in the gift shop. The books were captivating, as was the entire experience. But I was able to control my innate yearning to buy several titles. Proud of my financial constraint, I exited the shop with only three postcards. When I met Del at our prearranged place, he had in hand two handsome books (with handsome prices, of course). The coffee episode was still brewing inside me;

seeing those books he had bought really ticked me off. His blatant breach of contract stirred up the age-old issue of power and authority. But it simply did not seem appropriate to begin World War III at that moment, at that particular place, and over an eight-dollar bag of coffee, three cheap postcards, and two beautiful books (which I knew even then I would also enjoy).

Clearly at that moment, as I have many times throughout our quarter-of-a-century marriage, I understood that it is definitely a myth to think that money per se is the cause of most marital conflicts. The truth of the matter is that complex psychological issues are often more the reason for such haggling.

MYTH 20:

If You'll Just Communicate More, Your Marriage Will Be Better

NORM AND TONI talked to each other all the time. They communicated more than any other couple I have ever known. They shared every thought with each other, holding nothing back. They were completely honest with each other and seemed to thrive on total confession and unmasked emotions. Their marriage lasted seven years.

Norm and Toni fell victim to the myth that all you have to do is communicate more and you will have the perfect marriage. Many couples, like Norm and Toni, see *more communication* as the personal genie slithering out of Aladdin's lamp, empowered with the magic to smooth their marital path, solve all their problems, and bring true all their wishes for never-ending marital bliss. Unfortunately, this is a dangerous myth, bringing wrack and ruin to many marriages.

It is clearly not true that if you'll just communicate *more* with each other, your marriage will be better. The truth is, if you communicate *better* with each other, your marriage will be better. This is not merely a play on words; it is a harsh reality. In the case of communication, *quality* is probably more important than *quantity*, although a dynamic, satisfying marriage relationship does demand quantity, too. Meaningful communication simply cannot be compressed into little snatches of superficial chats.

Like Norm and Toni, numerous individuals sign the marriage contract blindly, assuming their intimate existence will be nourished by unending and unedited dialogue. They are astonished when it does not happen. Norm expressed what many have thought: "If you cannot let down and be yourself at home with your marriage partner, where can you?" Each partner, of course, should enjoy a certain sense of relaxation and freedom, but not in a way that kills a relationship. No lasting satisfaction is gained from that approach.

In this chapter, we'll look at several familiar expressions that cause misconceptions about communication. I hope this discussion will help you in your quest not just for *more* communication, but for *better* communication.

Practice Makes Perfect

"Practice makes perfect" is true only if you practice the right skills in the right way. The acid test for any skill is whether or not it helps accomplish your goal. If your goal is to create a harmonious, enjoyable, and dynamic relationship, then you should practice the communication skills that help you reach that goal.

Perhaps a negative example will illustrate this important point—so, back to our "most communicative" couple, Norm and Toni, who routinely practiced communication skills that split them apart. Norm, for example, constantly bombasted Toni with his sharp-tongued sarcasm. His skill of shredding Toni to ribbons was honed to perfection. Toni said of Norm, "He has a quick mind, and his cutting remarks go right to the bone." Another time she commented, "Norm is caustic. Watch out for the afterburn; you'll get

singed as he goes by." Norm offered similar remarks about
Toni—for example, "She needs a *tact* transfusion!"

In the beginning of their marriage, Norm and Toni were
well meaning and sincere. They plainly were victims of the
myth that *more* communication is better. And to them,
"more" meant being absolutely honest and saying exactly
what they felt like saying.

Their misguided thinking, like that of other well-intentioned individuals, stemmed partially from the "do-and-
say-what-you-feel-like" cure-all psychology popularized in
the 1960s and '70s. This psychology of individualism suggests you are violating your personal integrity if you behave in ways or say things you do not *feel*. Allowing mates
to say things to each other they would not even dream of
saying to a complete stranger, this psychology is extremely
damaging, as Norm and Toni's marriage failure illustrates.

Consider these small, everyday—and hurtful—scenarios;
then consider the better, more encouraging comments that
follow each scenario:

1. Toni was nervous about the meal she had prepared for
   the two couples she and Norm had invited to their house.
   As soon as the couples sat down to the table, Norm said,
   "Hope your stomachs are strong. Toni is not the world's
   best cook."

   *"I hope you will enjoy this meal. Toni has really worked hard
   at learning to cook."*

2. Norm had labored for days on a report he was scheduled
   to give at an important business meeting. One evening
   as he was going over his notes for the last time, Toni
   said, "I sure hope you don't put those important executives to sleep with all that!"

   *"I bet those executives will be impressed with all the time
   and effort you've put into your report!"*

3. Toni had gained some weight and was struggling to lose
   it. Norm knew she was extremely sensitive about the

extra pounds she had put on. While they were ordering lunch one day at a downtown restaurant, Norm said to Toni, "My gosh, no wonder you look like a pig; you eat like one!"

"You look great to me! But if you want to lose some weight, I want to help you. I'll have the salad bar, too."

In contrast to Norm and Toni, one couple agreed when they first got married twenty-five years ago to work at developing the communication skills that would build a strong marriage, one in which the Golden Rule of communication would be enforced: "Say unto others what you would have them say unto you." Here are some scriptures they say have helped them:

> May my spoken words and unspoken thoughts be pleasing even to you, O Lord my Rock and my Redeemer (Ps. 19:14, TLB).

> If anyone can control his tongue, it proves that he has perfect control over himself in every other way (James 3:2, TLB).

> He who guards his mouth and his tongue,
> Guards his soul from troubles (Prov. 21:23, NASB).

> A gentle answer turns away wrath,
> But a harsh word stirs up anger (Prov. 15:1, NASB).

> A soothing tongue is a tree of life,
> But perversion in it crushes the spirit (Prov. 15:4, NASB).

> Set a guard over my mouth, O Lord,
> keep watch over the door of my lips (Ps. 141:3, RSV).

When couples put these time-proven guidelines for communication into practice, their marriage is guaranteed to get better!

If You Can't Say Something Nice, Don't Say Anything at All

In general, it is pretty good advice that "If you can't say something nice, don't say anything at all." But carried to extreme, this approach is just not realistic. Two married people trying to balance all the intricacies and complexities of family life are going to disagree occasionally, and conflicts are inevitable. But effective communication can keep these disagreements from developing into open warfare or a cold war. I'm convinced that marriage partners need to address their differences head-on, perhaps with the pact, "If you have something you need to say, say it in a nice way."

Here are some ground rules my husband and I use to restore peace to the home front:

1. Talk calmly until we have identified the real issue that is bothering us. Avoid "chasing rabbits" or digging up bones of contention from the past. Keep blinders on so we can concentrate on just this one current issue or present problem and talk about definite steps we can take to solve it or at least work toward some resolution that both of us can live with.

2. Avoid attacking each other; focus attention on the problem. Do not resort to name calling, insulting, accusing, blaming, or over-generalizing ("You *never* . . ." or "You *always* . . ."). We try never to say something we'll later be sorry about, like, "I hate you," or "I wish I had never married you."

3. Hear each other out rather than "tuning each other out." Be willing to listen—really listen—to each other without interrupting or trying to defend our own position. Try to understand each other's point of view.

4. Speak for self; use "I" statements and not "You" statements. For example, avoid saying, "*You* make me so angry when you act like I should do all the housework," or "*You* never lift a finger around this house." Instead, use an "I" statement like, "I get so discouraged when I feel like you

expect me to do all the housework in addition to working full time."

5. Avoid sending double messages, that is, saying one thing when actions are saying another. Also avoid using kidding, flippant remarks that mask true feelings (I fall into this treacherous trap).

6. Avoid a self-righteous critical attitude. A little magnet of a butterfly is always on our refrigerator door; under the beautiful butterfly colors are the words "Love—Don't Criticize." Held by the magnet is a well-worn card with this reminder written on it: "Don't be too hard on me, for everybody makes misteaks, mistakes, mistaeks . . . oh well. Please love me like I am!"

7. Be willing to compromise. Recognize that no one human being can be 100 percent right all the time and that an attitude of give-and-take is a sign of maturity and strength, not weakness. An added bonus is that if one partner makes concessions or admits that the other has a legitimate complaint, the other generally reflects that same attitude. Identify positive actions each can take to restore peace and harmony.

Following these ground rules has helped us behave in ways that build mutual respect, not tear it down. At the same time, these rules have guided us through some potentially dangerous mine fields in our marriage without mortally wounding the self-esteem of either of us.

Another caution, though, about communication and conflict: Avoid the hazardous misconception that good communication will avoid or eliminate all conflict. Effective communication can, of course, diffuse conflict, and it is essential for working out problems and for working through crises. But communication even at its best will not miraculously dissolve all conflict.

Never Go to Bed Angry

Someone once said, "Old proverbs never die; they don't even fade away." One that has not faded but gained the status of Holy Writ is, "Never go to bed angry." Many mothers teach it to their daughters, marital advisers pass it on to their clients, and many happily married couples swear by it. Frankly, I do not think it holds up; my own marital experience debunks it completely. In fact, I cannot think of a *better* place than bed to go when you are angry at each other. The author of "Never Go to Bed Angry—And Other Myths about Marriage," agrees and explores some other possible places to go when you are angry:

> The kitchen? You'll just argue about who should get that last piece of chocolate cake. The den? You'll fight about which late-night TV show to turn on. The living room? That's probably where the battle started. Home to mother? Come on, you're too grown up for that.
>
> I think bed may be the very best place of all—especially if it's a double. There's something so ridiculous about that huffy back-to-back posture at the far edges of the mattress that one of you is almost certain to giggle—or fall out of bed. Since it's impossible to giggle and stay angry, you'll probably have to call a truce.[1]

"You Don't Understand"

Psychologists say one of the deepest needs is to understand and to be understood. Remember the last time you felt no one understood what you were feeling? Alone. Helpless. Fear. Emptiness. The burgeoning number of self-help groups of various kinds reflects this human yearning to "connect" with others who have had similar experiences and, subsequently, similar feelings and mutual understanding.

Nowhere are there any better guidelines for providing the setting or stage for authentic understanding than in 1 Corinthians 13, often called the Love Chapter. Love, it is pointed out, is patient and kind. It is not jealous or envious, and it is not "puffed up" or arrogant. Love is courteous and generous, not selfish. Love is not irritable or touchy but even-tempered. Love gives the benefit of the doubt. Love doesn't hold a grudge. Love is sincere, and it is unconditional. When these qualities of love are practiced in a marriage, a climate is created in which mutual understanding can develop.

When we understand the *why* of certain attitudes and behaviors, we are much more tolerant. I heard a story years ago illustrating this point. A man was standing at the side of a highway throwing clumps of mud at cars passing by. Finally one irate driver stopped, stepped from his car, and yelled, "Hey, man, what's the idea?" Before he could say anything else, the man throwing the mud said, "Thank you for stopping. I tried to wave others down, but no one would stop. My friend and I were hunting and he accidentally shot himself. He's over that hill . . . hurt bad. Please help me."

This story also illustrates another point: When people are acting their worst they usually need help—and understanding—the most.

"You Just Don't Appreciate Me"

William James, perhaps the world's greatest psychologist, wrote extensively, and his writings were profound but practical. Dealing with human nature, especially emotions that motivate and control human behavior, one of his books was hailed as a masterpiece. But he was heard to say some years after that book had enjoyed great acceptance that he had failed to discuss in it the most significant human craving of all—the deep, heartfelt yearning in each of us to be *appreciated*. How many times in your own marriage have you said to your mate (or at least felt it): "You just don't appreciate me"?

Appreciation can take thousands of forms in marriage. It can be a well-deserved compliment on some task well done. It can be a sincere, "Thank you for loving me." It can be a little bragging on your mate in front of his relatives and your in-laws: "You all did a good job rearing him. I'm glad I got him." A smile, a handclasp, and an arm around a shoulder can express appreciation.

Seeing all the things we could complain about in marriage or about our mate is easy. In contrast, a little extra

effort may have to be exerted to pinpoint and communicate
the things we appreciate. But it is worth the trouble. For
generally when the gift of appreciation is given, it returns
manifold. The experiences of numerous married couples
vouch for the validity of this ageless truth: "Give generously, for your gifts will return to you . . ." (Eccles. 11:1,
TLB).

Actions Speak Louder Than Words

Everything we do sends a message. The raising of eye-
brows, the slamming of a door, a warm smile, clinched fists.
The tapping of a pencil, the shrugging of shoulders, the
shedding of tears, a quick kiss on the cheek. Experts estimate that fifty to 100 bits of information are exchanged
each second between communicating individuals. Even doing nothing, even silence can speak volumes. "The cruelest
lies," said Robert Louis Stevenson, "are often told in silence." The power of silence is also captured in this familiar
rhyme:

> Sticks and stones are hard on bones
>   and aimed with angry art.
> Words can sting like anything
> But silence breaks the heart.

The saying, "Actions speak louder than words," has a
great deal of truth in it, but in marriage, as in all interper-
sonal relationships, we need to be careful how we interpret
those actions. Early in our marriage I avoided conflict any
way I could. Sometimes that meant going into another room
without saying anything. Del interpreted my nonverbal behavior as my being angry. At other times he interpreted that
same behavior as indifference. Both interpretations were
wrong, and the consequences could have been quite damaging to our relationship. But Del was wise enough to ask
me what my actions meant. And that's exactly what needs
to be done when nonverbal behavior is puzzling or is inconsistent with the words used.

Most married couples experience many instances when
the message received is not the intended message. A wife
may have had a demanding day with the children, or an
exasperating day on the job, and be completely exhausted
when she and her husband go to bed. When the husband
embraces her, she turns over and yawns. Before she says
anything, he feels rejected simply by her actions. Words are
needed to clarify what the nonverbal behavior really
means: "Honey, I really love you—and need you—but I am
so tired I just want to go to sleep." If the husband was not
suggesting sex, as she had assumed, this also gives him the
opportunity to say: "I'm tired, too. I just wanted to let you
know that I love you."

Interpreting what the other really means, whether in
nonverbal communication or with words, is one of the
challenges of understanding each other. No infallible way
exists to do this. But one of the most effective tools for
communicating satisfactorily is to simply ask your mate
what is meant by words or actions when you are unsure
of their meaning. Avoid guessing and always rely on this
time-proven wisdom that is the tap root of all communication:

> Most important of all continue to show deep love for each
> other, for love makes up for many of your faults (1 Pet. 4:8,
> TLB).

"I Am Afraid to Tell You How I Really Feel"

Some couples operate under the myth that happily married people never unload personal problems on their
spouses. David Mace of Black Mountain, North Carolina, a
longtime family-relations consultant, estimates that among
85 percent of the couples he has worked with, at least one
partner was stewing about something without telling the
other. The problem, he says, is that people are afraid of
appearing vulnerable to their mates. "But the deepest intimacy grows out of opening up and letting your partner
know you need him or her," say Mace.

Consider the case of the Hudsons. Jean resented Bob's spending every weekend running errands for his aging parents. At first she felt guilty about being jealous of two elderly people who were unable to manage their own affairs. She finally admitted to Bob, "I am afraid to tell you how I really feel." He encouraged Jean to be honest, for he had known for some time that something was bothering her. After Jean told Bob how she felt, he admitted that he, too, resented the time his parents required—partly because it prevented him from spending more time with his two teenage children.

Once they had openly shared their feelings, Bob and Jean were able to work out a solution. Jean agreed to help Bob with his parents. And when Bob and Jean's teen-agers recognized the problem, they, too, began to help. The situation could not be changed; but open, honest discussions eased the Hudsons' tensions and allowed them to consider options for handling the problem more satisfactorily. "What could have destroyed our marriage ended up drawing the family closer together," Jean concludes.

"It Goes in One Ear and out the Other"

As a young child when I apparently had not listened to something said to me or had not heeded it, I can remember being admonished, "It goes in one ear and out the other." Unfortunately, many of us carry into adulthood and into our marriages this infantile, ineffective ability to pay attention, to really listen. We erroneously think listening is a passive activity. It is not. Effective listening—being a successful *receiver* of a message sent to us—demands paying close attention to the words spoken, the tone and quality of the voice, the depth of meaning in the sender's eyes, the facial expression, and the body movements.

Above all, listening requires something our daughter Christi put into words when she was about ten and was pouring out a problem to me. When I nonchalantly commented that I could not understand why she was so upset, she instructed me, "Listen to me *with your heart*." I have

found that is good advice not only for meaningful parent-
child communication but also for husband-wife heart-to-
heart talks. When someone's words take a detour through
your heart, it sure keeps them from "going in one ear and
out the other."

"You Should Know by Now . . ."

Expecting your marriage partner to know your thoughts,
whether you are genuinely sorry about a wrong committed
or you simply feel a sudden surge of longing for love and
attention, is a precipitous presumption. I have heard otherwise intelligent individuals say dumb things like these:

"If you really loved me, you would know how I feel."

"I shouldn't have to tell you; you should know what I
    think about that."

"You know I love you; I don't need to tell you all the
    time."

No one, no matter how clairvoyant, can automatically
know the thoughts and feelings of another, regardless of
the intensity of love and devotion. Experience teaches it is
best to say what you mean, mean what you say, and to not
expect your marriage partner to read your mind. Most importantly, remember it is not *more* communication but
rather *quality* communication that has the power to bring
joy to your marriage:

> *Like apples of gold in settings of silver, so is a word
> spoken at the right moment.*

> —Proverbs 25:11, NASB

MYTH 21:

It's the Quality of Time,
Not the Quantity of Time,
You Spend with Each Other
That Matters

MY WIFE AND I took one of those weekend marriage enrichment seminars," explained one husband. "Two questions hit us hard," he continued. "The leader asked us to
estimate how many minutes we spent in taking out the
garbage each week. We didn't know what was coming, so
we answered truthfully: 'About five minutes a day or
thirty-five minutes a week.' Then she asked us about how
many minutes a day did we as a couple spend in face-to-
face conversation with full attention given to each other.
You guessed it! The *garbage* got more time and attention."
The husband concluded, "We're fooling ourselves if we
think that five minutes a day is enough to maintain a marriage. And it certainly isn't enough to make the marriage
grow."[1]

In many marriages, numerous things get more time and
attention than marriage partners. Whether it's daily tasks,

like taking out the garbage; career-related activities; or merely watching television, reading the newspaper, and pursuing personal hobbies, there is fierce competition for the time that marriage partners might otherwise spend with one another. As our days together flick by in rapid succession, a debate rages over whether we need *quality* time or *quantity* of time with loved ones. And even though this debate most often centers on parents' time with children, it's just as controversial when applied to marriages.

To defend one idea or the other—or both—analogies from other areas of life are frequently offered. For instance, marriage is like a garden, some people say. Tend it carefully, water it, nurture it, weed it to eliminate the undesirable, take dutiful measures against injurious insects, and you will have a lush garden of flowers, fruits, or vegetables to enjoy. Neglect a garden, and you will have a withered, insect-ridden, rotten mess overgrown with troublesome weeds. The point is this: You get out of a relationship what you put into it.

Not satisfied with folksy analogies, Dr. Nick Stinnett and Dr. John DeFrain of the University of Nebraska conducted a comprehensive research project to identify the qualities of strong families. Over 90 percent of these "strong" couples said they spend "a great deal of time together."

Conversely, divorced couples interviewed usually spent little time together before their breakup. These researchers contend that couples who choose quality of time over quantity are often either consciously or subconsciously avoiding genuine intimacy. As one woman who has enjoyed thirty years of marriage puts it, "Heartfelt conversations and meaningful time together simply cannot be squeezed into little snatches of minutes here and there."

What Makes a Happy Family?

"What do you think makes a happy family?" Over 1,500 children were asked this question in a survey. The children did not list fine homes, cars, money, or any of the things that money can buy. The answer they gave most frequently was *doing things together!* This answer reminds me of when I was attending graduate school at Mills College in Oakland, California. It was 1963, a year branded indelibly on the minds of many in that area, for it marked the beginning of the "free speech movement" and the student denouncement of materialistic values of their parents and society in general. But I remember even more vividly University of California Chancellor Clark Kerr's concise but meaning-packed statement to the parents of the protesting students and to parents in general: "Spend time on your kids, not money."

This is good advice anytime, anyplace, and it applies equally well to marriage partners, who may need to be reminded from time to time to spend *quality* time with each other—in a large *quantity.* The fact is that good marriages aren't the result of quality *or* quantity of time. They're the result of *both!*

Consider this illustration about a steak used by family therapist George Rekers to make clear the relationship between quality and quantity:

> . . . imagine you've gone to a new gourmet restaurant and that you decide to treat yourself to the best steak even though it costs $18.00. The steak arrives on an expensive china plate, served with flair by an impeccably dressed waiter. You note with shock and dismay that the steak is a one-inch cube. In horror, you question the waiter, who assures you that quality is what counts and this steak is *the best.* But if you're very hungry, you know that quantity also counts.[2]

Almost every study on family stress puts time pressures near the top. One reason time pressures need to be addressed is that they generate and intensify other stresses. When marriage partners suffer from too little time together, their communication suffers. And when communication suffers, the partners are less likely to deal effectively with other issues like financial concerns, problems with children, a mutually satisfying sex life, and getting all the work done around the house. Working out congenial agreements about all the nuts and bolts required to keep the massive machinery of marriage chugging along with no major breakdown requires time—lots of time.

Pollster Louis Harris studied more than 1,100 marriage partners who both worked outside the home and found that 26 percent of them felt a lack of time with each other. Four major time stressors were indicated:

Insufficient Couple Time (Women 50 percent; Men 52 percent)

Insufficient Family Play Time (Women 37 percent; Men 29 percent)

Insufficient "Me" Time (Women 40 percent; Men 29 percent)

Over-Scheduled Family Calendar (Women 32 percent; Men 39 percent)

What aspects of the time crunch are major stressors in your marriage?

Benjamin Franklin said, "Time is money," a saying readily affirmed in today's business world. What we need, however, is a similar saying emphasizing the immeasurable value of time to a marriage relationship. Family expert Dolores Curran points out that couples who have the most control and least stress over the issue of time are those who do indeed recognize it as a resource that needs the same attention as money. So they use techniques in managing time that are similar to the ones they use to manage their money: talking about it and sharing feelings and needs that arise from insufficient personal, couple, and family time; allocating time for certain activities; budgeting time; and prioritizing activities that eat up time.[3]

Taking the First Steps

In the book *We Never Have Time Just for Us,* author Wayne Rickerson points out that recognition of neglect is the first crucial step to remedying a suffering couple relationship. He points out that we do not go into marriage thinking, "Now our plan is to have fun and excitement, share goals and interests for the first two years, and then neglect these areas." But we invite neglect into our marriage when we do not *plan* ways to have fun and excitement, share interests, and set common goals.

People often commit themselves to the *idea* of change, but not the *effort* of change, says Dr. William Knaus in his book *How to Conquer Your Frustrations*. Dr. Knaus suggests that partners who are committed to carry out the effort will assess their situation, carefully identify achievable goals, formulate plans, organize for action, and then—most importantly—put the plans into action. All the plans in the world do little good if no action is taken on them. An old Russian proverb expresses it this way:

> You can study the map for years, but you don't get one step closer to the city until you start moving.

Our good friends Dennis and Sandi took that first step: They openly recognized their problem. What time they spent together was quality time, but there simply was not enough of it. So they set a goal to spend more time together. Of course, this was not as easy as it sounds.

Dennis is definitely a "people person," and as a pastor he was constantly in demand to counsel troubled couples, to comfort grieving families, and to meet myriad other human needs. He found he was spending more and more evenings meeting needs of his parishioners. Despite his efforts to share his time with Sandi and their children, enough hours simply did not exist. Family time suffered; Dennis and Sandi both knew something had to change.

"We *are* going to spend more time together," Sandi and Dennis both agreed. With pencils and calendar in hand, they set aside certain times throughout the week just for the two of them, including one dinner date a week. Dennis said, "At first it was really hard to turn people down and to tell them I was spending that time with Sandi. But then I found out that people's schedules were flexible; I could meet with them another time. In addition, Sandi and I were setting a good example for other couples. Our friends started spending more time together as couples. Now our marriage is improving, and so are the marriages of our friends and the members of our church."

Why Togetherness Dwindles in Marriage

When two people fall in love, they are inseparable. Every moment they can, they spend together. This pattern of togetherness and companionship usually continues into the early stages of marriage. Then what happens? Why do these two who felt so drawn to each other spend less and less time together? According to marriage expert Dr. Larry Halter, three factors account for couples' togetherness dwindling: child rearing, career climbing, and negative pressure. In *Traits of a Happy Couple* he says that *the first factor which robs couple time is childrearing responsibilities.*

After my youngest sister and her husband were killed by a drunk driver, their baby was adopted by another sister and brother-in-law—Brenda and Ron—who have provided marvelous love as well as additional brothers and a sister. Both in their parenting and in their marriage, Brenda and Ron truly reflect the wisdom in this anonymous poem:

> Cleaning and scrubbing
>   Can wait 'til tomorrow,
> For babies grow up,
>   We've learned to our sorrow—
> So quiet down, cobwebs,
>   Dust, go to sleep—
> I'm rocking my baby,
> And babies don't keep.

Ron and Brenda know that babies don't keep. But they also know that marriages don't keep either. So they plan as carefully for couple time as they do for parenting time. Grandparents sometimes care for the children while Brenda accompanies Ron on his coaching weekends. Sometimes Brenda and another sister, Martha, who has two children, trade baby-sitting favors to have some time alone with their husbands.

"Ron and I both love our children, but we know that the best thing we can give them is a set of parents who love each other and have a strong marriage," says Brenda. "We also know we cannot wait until the kids are grown and gone for us to spend time together. It takes a lot of planning, but having couple time together is the best investment we can make for ourselves and our children."

Career-climbing is the second factor that interferes with quality and quantity time together as a couple. The increasing number of women who work outside the home doubles the pressure careers put on couple time. Unfortunately, our society programs us to think in terms of success in the world of work outside the home. In so many subtle ways—and some not so subtle—we are influenced to believe that getting a good job and making money are more important than developing a good marriage. Husbands and wives must tenaciously guard against their careers crowding out their couple time.

Coercion and negative pressure tactics comprise a third reason couple time is eroded. Dr. Halter explains how pleasing behaviors—actions which bond two individuals together in the first place—begin to decrease, and displeasing, annoying behaviors—which were overlooked during courtship— begin to increase as time goes by. He says that naturally you want individuals to restore the pleasing behaviors and eliminate the displeasing ones. But most people lack the skills to solve these problems in positive ways; they resort to coercive tactics, like criticism, and negative pressures, like the silent treatment, to change their mate. The result of these coercive and negative tactics is alienation—and a decrease in both quality and quantity of time.[4]

An additional reason many couples suffer from lack of *quality* time together is that our Puritan heritage with its strong work ethic makes us think we should not relax and enjoy ourselves—or our mate—until our work is done. The reality, of course, is that all our work is never going to be done. If we postpone pleasurable time together, we will find ourselves on a treadmill with nothing pleasurable to anticipate—in a rat race that no one ever wins.

Planned, Not Mechanical

Happy marriages generally are characterized by a lot of quality time; but the togetherness of the mates is not stifling, and it is planned but not mechanical. Says one wife, "The balance between *sufficient* and *stifling* for togetherness is different for different couples, and it is different for each couple at different times."

Couples who have quality time plan for it. They scrutinize their activities with an eye for paring them down. They drop their membership in many clubs and organizations. They learn to say no to school, church, and community leaders who ask them to volunteer for activities that will take away from family time. They learn to live with lower housekeeping standards. They do not strive to have a perfect lawn. Like Dennis and Sandi, they learn to feel more confident in being able to say, "No, we are going to spend that time with our family."

Activities Couples Enjoy Together

Secrets of Strong Families summarizes the activities partners from strong marriages enjoy together:

Meals—Many mentioned the enjoyment of eating meals together. One mother said, "We eat the evening meal together. In extreme cases, one of us may not be there, but everyone knows that being absent from dinner is not taken lightly. We use that time to share triumphs and tribulations. In a hectic world we need some common ground where we can meet." Another said, "We always eat dinner together and try to be together for breakfast as well. And we have a rule of no television during meals."

House and Yard Work—Strong families have learned to make the time necessary for running a household into an opportunity to get together and to communicate. Some of their comments illustrate: "I work until late in the afternoon, so I need help getting dinner ready . . . . We all get in the kitchen and talk about what went on at school and work while we fix dinner."

Outdoor Activities—A large number of the strong marriage partners mentioned outdoor activities as favorite ways to be together. Many play catch or yard games. They camp, canoe, hike, picnic, stargaze, play league sports, bicycle, walk, and swim. Their responses give some clues to the allure of the outdoors: "We love to canoe a little river not far from here. After a day of sunlight on the leaves, fresh air, the ripple of the water, my soul is refreshed. My husband says he feels more in touch with the eternally important things. He gains perspective; petty trials come and go but the river flows on. The kids have a blast swimming, collecting rocks, hunting fossils, and chasing frogs."

Another spouse describes this favorite getaway: "We have a special town on the Gulf Coast that is a favorite of ours. We camp and fish and go crabbing. There are no phones or television. For a couple of days the outside world disappears. What a pleasure it is to get up when we want, eat when we're hungry, and be free of schedules."

Indoor Recreation—Playing board games like Monopoly or Scrabble, putting together puzzles, watching selected TV programs, and eating popcorn were all mentioned as fun things to do together.

Church, Synagogue, School—For many strong families, weekly worship is a family event. Also, activities at school, scouting, or 4-H often involve the entire family as well. If the children have a band concert, recital, or are in a program, Mom and Dad and the family are in the audience.

Special Events—These include holidays, vacations, and personal observances such as birthdays. One person comments: "Birthdays are big events at our home. We have a special meal and cake. The birthday person gets presents, of course. We also have added our own twist. The birthday person gives small presents to family members as a way of thanking them for enriching his [her] life.[5]

If couples spend a lot of time together that is filled with squabbling, condescension, and hostility, nothing is gained. *Quantity* of time must be filled with *quality* interaction for the marriage relationship to be enhanced. In *Love Life for Every Married Couple* the authors admit that every couple's plan for sharing will be different. "Just make sure you have a plan," they emphasize, because "the natural tendency is to go your separate ways."[6]

A Blue Chip Investment

Step out in the open, never again to hide behind the misleading myth that "It's the quality of time, not the quantity of time, you spend with each other that matters." Make a commitment right now to spend more time with your partner than you do in taking out the garbage. Vow to "serve" your mate more than a one-inch cube of *quality* time.

Time is a blue chip investment for marriage relationships. Invested in both quality and quantity, it pays invaluable and lasting dividends.

ENDNOTES

MYTH 1: *All You Need Is Love*

1. Elaine Walster and G. William Walster, *A New Look at Love* (Reading, MA: Addison-Wesley, 1978), 108.
2. Marlene Shelton LaRoe and Lee Herrick, *How Not to Ruin a Perfectly Good Marriage* (New York: Bantam, 1980), 129.
3. David Field, *Marriage Personalities* (Eugene, OR: Harvest House, 1986), 164.
4. Paul A. Mickey with William Proctor, "All Stressed Up and Some Place to Go," *Marriage Partnership*, Winter 1990, 62.

MYTH 2: *The Key to a Happy Marriage Is Choosing the Right Mate*

1. Sidney J. Harris, *On the Contrary* (Boston: Houghton Mifflin Co., 1962), 323.

MYTH 3: *Marriage Stifles Individuality*

1. Anne Morrow Lindbergh as quoted in James Leslie McCrary, *Freedom and Growth in Marriage* (New York: John Wiley and Sons, 1980), ix.
2. Paul Tournier as quoted in Hazen G. Werner, *The Bible and the Family* (Nashville: Abingdon Press, 1966), 30.

MYTH 4: *Spouses Must Be Compatible*

1. Ruth Graham, "Needed: Incompatibility," *Christianity Today* 25, no. 16:25.
2. Chuck and Barb Snyder, *Incompatibility: Grounds for a Great Marriage!* (Phoenix: Questar Publishers, Inc., 1988), 9–10.

MYTH 5: *Marriage Partners Need to Look for Weaknesses in Their Marriage and Fix Them*

1. Paul Faulkner, *Making Things Right When Things Go Wrong* (Fort Worth, TX: Sweet Publishing, 1986), 111.
2. Robert Schuller, *Eight Words of Wisdom for Husbands and Wives!* (Garden Grove, CA: Robert Schuller Ministries, 1987), 8–10.
3. *Daily Guideposts 1988* (Carmel, NY: Guideposts, 1987), 9.

MYTH 6: *Variety Is the Spice of Life and of Marriage*

1. Interview with Andy Walker, Associate Pastor for Singles, First Baptist Church, Woodway, TX, 21 November 1989.

MYTH 7: *Marriage Is Serious Business*

1. T. A. Bryant and others, compilers, *Today's Dictionary of the Bible* (Carmel, NY: Guideposts), 361.
2. Phyllis McGinley from "Laughter in Our Family" as quoted in *The New Catholic Treasure of Wit and Humor*, Paul Bussard, ed. (New York: Meredith Press, 1968), 195.
3. Virginia Stir, *Peoplemaking* (Palo Alto, CA: Science and Behavior Books, Inc., 1972), 11–12.
4. Barbara Russell Chesser, *Because You Care: Practical Ideas for Helping Those Who Grieve* (Waco, TX: Word Books, 1988), 50.
5. Ibid., 51–52.
6. Elton Trueblood, *The Humor of Christ* (New York: Harper and Row, 1964), 127.

MYTH 8: *Families Are Falling Apart Because Women Are Working Outside the Home*

1. Eli Ginzberg as quoted in "How You Going to Get 'Em Back in the Kitchen? (You Aren't)," *Forbes*, 15 November 1977, 177.
2. Nancy Barcus, *Help Me, God, I'm a Working Mother!* (Valley Forge, PA: Judson Press, 1982), 62.

MYTH 9: *Good Sex Makes a Good Marriage*

1. Barbara Chesser, "Cathedral Sex," *Journal of Religion and Health*, 18, no. 1, January 1979, 38–48.

2. Charlie Shedd and Martha Shedd, *Celebration in the Bedroom* (Waco, TX: Word Books, 1981), 92. Used by permission.

MYTH 10: *Couples Need to Plan More for the Future*

1. Barbara Chesser, "Let's Go Bug Hunting More Often!" *Today's Christian Parent,* August 1983, 31.
2. From an interview with Frank Gentsch. Used by permission.

MYTH 11: *Wedding Rituals Are Just for Show*

1. Carle C. Zimmerman, *Family and Civilization* (New York: Harper and Brothers, 1947), 776.
2. Charles Thompson, *The Hand of Destiny* (London: Rider & Co., 1932), 49.
3. Barbara Chesser, "Analysis of Wedding Rituals: An Attempt to Make Weddings More Meaningful," *Family Relations* 29 (1980):205.
4. L. Eichler, *The Customs of Mankind* (New York: Doubleday, 1924), 188–190.
5. Peter Lacey, *The Wedding* (New York: Grosset & Dunlap, 1969), 270.
6. T. Sharper Knowlson, *The Origins of Popular Superstitions and Customs* (London: T. Werner Laruier Clifford's Inn, 1910), 101.
7. M. Seligson, *The Eternal Bliss Machine* (New York: Morrow, 1973), 21.
8. Lacey, 255.

MYTH 12: *Holidays Are Joyous Times That Bring Family Members Closer to Each Other*

1. Dan Hurley, "Beat the Holiday Blues," *Private Clubs,* November–December 1988, 34.
2. Ibid.
3. Ibid.
4. Gloria Gaither and Shirley Dobson, *Let's Make a Memory* (Waco, TX: Word Books, 1983), 11.
5. Ann Landers, *The Los Angeles Times* and Creators Syndicates. Used by permission.
6. Dan Hurley, "Beat the Holiday Blues," *Private Clubs,* November–December 1988, 35. Used with permission of the author.

MYTH 13: *High Standards Create Highly Satisfying Marriages*

1. Richard Farson, "Why Good Marriages Fail," *McCall's*, October 1971, 110.
2. Harold LeCrone, "'All-or-nothing' Outlook Harmful," *Waco Tribune-Herald*, 26 February 1989, 2B.
3. Harold LeCrone, "'Perfect Couple's,' Marriage Falters," *Waco Tribune-Herald*, 10 July 1988, 2B.
4. James C. Dobson, *Straight Talk to Men and Their Wives* (Waco, TX: Word Books, 1980), 94.
5. Charles R. Swindoll, *Dropping Your Guard* (Waco, TX: Word Books, 1983), 152–53.
6. Frederick Herwaldt, Jr., "The Ideal Relationship and Other Myths about Marriage," *Christianity Today*, 9 April 1982, 30.
7. Jan Halper, "Male Mystique," *American Way*, August 1989, 42–44.

MYTH 14: *Hard Times Bring Marriage Partners Closer Together*

1. Barbara Chesser, "Families in Crises: Accidental Killers—Impact on Individual and Family Relationships," research project at University of Nebraska-Lincoln to be published by Lexington Books, DC Heath and Company, co-authored with Gwen Gilliam.
2. Carolyn Jabs, "Making Hard Times Work for Your Marriage," *Reader's Digest*, August 1989, 147.
3. Morton Hunt, "Is *Your* Family Crisis-Proof?" *Families*, November 1981, 13.
4. Barbara Russell Chesser, *Because You Care: Practical Ideas for Helping Those Who Grieve* (Waco, TX: Word Books, 1988).

MYTH 15: *Signs of Impending Failure Are Easy to Detect*

1. Carl Wesley, "The Divorced Personality," *Psychology Today*, January 1987, 66.
2. Alfie Kohn, "Making the Most of Marriage," *Psychology Today*, December 1987, 6.
3. Nick Stinnett and John DeFrain, *Secrets of Strong Families* (New York: Berkley Books, 1986), 17–122.
4. Donald R. Harvey, *The Drifting Marriage: The Most Common Cause of Marital Failure among Christian Couples* (Old Tappan, NJ: Fleming H. Revell Co., 1988), 11.
5. Ibid., 215–216.

MYTH 16: *Divorce Lets You Begin a Fresh New Life*

1. Paul A. Mickey and William Proctor, *Tough Marriage: How to Make a Difficult Relationship Work* (New York: William Morrow and Co., 1986), 28.
2. Interview with Dr. Judith Wallerstein, 14 January 1984.
3. Dean Merrill, *Clergy Couples in Crisis* (Waco, TX: Word Books, 1985), 12.
4. Mel Krantzler, *Creative Divorce* (New York: Signet, 1974), 12.

MYTH 17: *If You Really Love Me . . .* *(The Myth of Conditional Love)*

1. Dr. Avodah K. Offit as quoted in "Six Myths about Extramarital Affairs," by Alice Fleming, *Reader's Digest,* October 1982, 63.
2. Arthur Maslow also quoted in "Six Myths about Extramarital Affairs," *Reader's Digest,* 66.
3. Dr. Avodah K. Offit as quoted in "Six Myths about Extramarital Affairs," *Reader's Digest,* 66.
4. Ibid.
5. Interview with Dr. John DeFrain, 2 June 1989.
6. Norman Lobsenz, "What Makes a Marriage as Good as Gold?" *Family Weekly,* 6 February 1983, 25.
7. Arnold A. Lazarus, *Marital Myths* (San Luis Obispo, CA: Impact Publishers, 1985), 53.
8. Diana S. Richmond Garland and David E. Garland, *Beyond Companionship — Christians in Marriage* (Philadelphia: The Westminster Press, 1986), 13–14.

MYTH 18: *Anger Has No Place in Marriage*

1. Carlfred Broderick as quoted in "Five Myths That Can Wreck Your Marriage," Barbara Chesser, *Reader's Digest,* June 1984, 24.
2. From William J. Lederer and Donald D. Jackson, *The Mirages of Marriage,* as quoted in Nick Stinnett and James Walters, *Relationships in Marriage and the Family* (New York: Macmillan, 1977), 54.
3. Arnold P. Goldstein and Alan Rosenbaum, *Aggress-Less: How to Turn Anger and Aggression into Positive Action* (Englewood Cliffs, NJ: Prentice-Hall, 1982), 34–39.

MYTH 19: *Spouses Argue Most over Money (and Sex)*

1. James E. Kilgore, *Try Marriage Before Divorce* (Waco, TX: Word Books, 1978), 41.
2. H. Norman Wright, *Making Peace with Your Partner* (Dallas: Word Publishing, 1988), 111.
3. Caroline Bailey, *A Loving Conspiracy* (London: Quartet Books, 1984), 167.
4. Ruth Stafford Peale, "How to Have a 'Good' Argument," *Plus: The Magazine of Positive Thinking* 40, no. 6 (part II):24.

MYTH 20: *If You'll Just Communicate More, Your Marriage Will Be Better*

1. Jennifer L. Barrett, "Never Go to Bed Angry—And Other Myths about Marriage," *Woman's Day,* 9 September 1983, 63.

MYTH 21: *It's the Quality of Time, Not the Quantity of Time, You Spend with Each Other That Matters*

1. Nick Stinnett and John DeFrain, *Secrets of Strong Families* (New York: Berkley Books, 1986), 83.
2. George Rekers as quoted in Stinnett and DeFrain, *Secrets of Strong Families,* 83.
3. Dolores Curran, "Secrets for Finding Extra Hours in Your Day," *Marriage Partnership,* Winter 1989, 82.
4. Larry L. Halter, *Traits of a Happy Couple* (Waco, TX: Word Books, 1988), 163–165.
5. Stinnett and DeFrain, *Secrets of Strong Families,* 91–93. Used by permission.
6. Ed Wheat and Gloria Okes Perkins, *Love Life for Every Married Couple* (Grand Rapids, MI: Zondervan Publishing House, 1980), 190.

APPENDIX:

Suggested Reading

Babbage, S. B. *Christianity and Sex.* Chicago: Inter-varsity Press, 1967.

Cooper, Darien. *You Can Be the Wife of a Happy Husband.* Wheaton, IL: Victory Books, SP Publications Inc., 1984.

Dobson, James. *What Wives Wish Their Husbands Knew About Women.* Wheaton, IL: Tyndale House Publishers, 1975.

Drakeford, J. W. *Made for Each Other.* Nashville, TN: Broadman Press, 1973.

Guernsey, Dennis. *Thoroughly Married.* Waco, TX: Word Books, 1975.

Harrell, I. and A. Harrell. *The Opposite Sex.* Waco, TX: Word Books, 1972.

Howell, J. C. *Teaching About Sex: A Christian Approach.* Nashville, TN: Broadman Press, 1966.

LaHaye, Tim and Beverly LaHaye. *The Act of Marriage.* Grand Rapids, MI: Zondervan Publishing House, 1976.

McDonald, Dick and Paula McDonald. *Loving Free.* New York: Ballantine Books, 1973.

Meredith, Don. *Becoming One.* Nashville, TN: Thomas Nelson Publishers, 1979.

Merrill, Dean. *How to Really Love Your Wife.* Grand Rapids, MI: Zondervan Publishing House, 1980.

Miles, Herbert J. *Sexual Happiness in Marriage.* Grand Rapids, MI: Zondervan Publishing House, 1967.

Narramore, Clyde. *Life and Love: A Christian View of Sex.* Grand Rapids, MI: Zondervan Publishing House, 1974.

Penner, Clifford and Joyce Penner. *The Gift of Sex: A Christian Guide to Sexual Fulfillment.* Waco, TX: Word, Inc., 1981.

Rice, Shirley. *Physical Unity in Marriage.* Norfolk, VA: The Tabernacle Church of Norfolk, 1973.

Small, Dwight H. *Christian: Celebrate Your Sexuality.* Old Tappan, NJ: Fleming H. Revell, 1974.

Smedes, Lewis B. *Sex for Christians*. Grand Rapids, MI: Wm. B. Eerdmans Publishing Co., 1976.

Short, Ray E. *Sex, Love, or Infatuation*. Minneapolis, MN: Augsburg Publishing House, 1978.

Strauss, Richard L. *Marriage Is for Love*. Wheaton, IL: Tyndale House Publishers, 1973.

Timmons, Tim. *One Plus One*. Washington, DC: Canon Press, 1974.

Trobisch, Ingrid. *The Joy of Being a Woman*. New York: Harper & Row Publishers, 1975.

Vincent, M. O. *God, Sex and You*. New York: J. B. Lippincott Company, 1971.

Wheat, Ed and Gloria Okes Perkins. *Love Life for Every Married Couple*. Grand Rapids, MI: Zondervan Publishing House, 1980.

Wheat, Ed, and Gaye Wheat. *Intended for Pleasure: Sex Technique and Sexual Fulfillment in Christian Marriage*. Old Tappan, NJ: Fleming H. Revell, 1977.

Wright, Norman H. and J. J. Penner. *In Touch with Each Other: A Couple's Guide to Marital Communication*. Chicago: David C. Cook, 1976.